AGAINST DECONSTRUCTION

Against Deconstruction

John M. Ellis

PRINCETON UNIVERSITY PRESS

PRINCETON, NEW JERSEY

Published by Princeton University Press, 41 William Street,
Princeton, New Jersey 08540
In the United Kingdom: Princeton University Press,
Guildford, Surrey

Publication of this book has been aided by the Whitney Darrow
Fund of Princeton University Press

This book has been composed in Linotron Sabon

Clothbound editions of Princeton University Press books are
printed on acid-free paper, and binding materials are chosen for
strength and durability. Paperbacks, although satisfactory
for personal collections, are not usually suitable
for library rebinding

Printed in the United States of America by Princeton
University Press, Princeton, New Jersey

LIBRARY OF CONGRESS CATALOGING-IN-PUBLICATION DATA
Ellis, John M. (John Martin), 1936–
Against deconstruction / by John M. Ellis.
p. cm.
Bibliography: p.
Includes index.
ISBN 0-691-06754-6 (alk. paper)
1. Deconstruction. 2. Criticism. 3. Languages—Philosophy. I. Title.
PN98.D43E45 1989
801'.95—dc19   88-14045

Contents

Preface

DURING the last fifteen years, deconstruction has become an influential position in literary criticism and theory, and the name of its progenitor, Jacques Derrida, is now heard more often than any other in theoretical discussion. I have heard it said many times during this period that deconstruction was now on the wane, but to judge by what is being published, these comments reflect more wishful thinking than accurate observation: books and articles in the deconstructionist mode continue to appear at an ever increasing rate, and Derrida continues to be cited more than any other theorist. Meanwhile the very language of criticism has been influenced by deconstruction: talk of privileged ideas and of demystification, for example, is no longer restricted to deconstructionists.

Influential new theories usually spark a free and lively discussion, and I should like to think of this book simply as a contribution to a debate of that kind, which in more normal circumstances it might be. But at the moment a debate scarcely exists: books and articles that use and advocate deconstruction are abundant, but apart from a handful of reviews and review articles there is very little in print that might represent the anti-deconstructionist side of the debate. Any sense of a continuing dialogue and interchange between the two sides is completely lacking. This is surely very strange, given deconstruction's prominence. And it is regrettable—or ought to be—whatever position one might wish to take on the issues. New ideas are refined and sharpened in the course of the debate between those who introduce them and those who resist their introduction. This process of development and redefinition through coming to terms with adverse criticism is an essential one for the clarification of any new idea. The relation between the two sides is in some ways like that of predator and prey: the attention of the predator is unwelcome but also essential for the long term health of the species.

Why then does the usual exchange between proponents and

opponents barely exist in this case? Much of the answer must surely be found in the fact that deconstructionists have generally reacted with hostility and even outrage to any serious criticism of deconstruction and thus to any possibility of an exchange with their intellectual opponents. Given this initial response, it is almost inevitable that any riposte will be aimed, not at the argument that has been made, but at the credentials and motives of opponents; and, not uncommonly, this has resulted in deconstructionists seeming to want to set standards for participation in the debate that would effectively exclude skeptics from it. Critics are taken to task, for example, for making criticisms of particular deconstructive arguments without having first immersed themselves in and having rehearsed their knowledge of the full range of deconstructive writings or for showing insufficient sympathy for deconstruction to demonstrate their credibility. Both points might, of course, be made legitimately *after* an analysis of the opposing argument had shown how distortions and misconceptions had entered into it because of insufficient acquaintance with a broad range of deconstructive writings or because of uncontrolled antipathy; but their use as reasons sufficient in themselves for ignoring a counterargument would be unimaginable in any other sphere of inquiry. Take an example from philosophy. Wittgenstein's private language argument is debated endlessly by those who think it of profound significance and those who think it a pernicious error and by those who have made the study of Wittgenstein their life's work as well as those who have no interest in him whatever aside from the issues raised by this particular argument. Regardless of the great diversity of these contributions to the printed discussion, each is judged by the same standard: Did it throw any new light on the inherent logic of the private language argument? The background or disposition of the individual contributor is a secondary issue only likely to be reached, if at all, after the primary judgment has been made on the logic of the contribution. In the unlikely event that anyone were to insist that only those who were sympathetic to Wittgenstein, or who set their analysis of this one issue in the context of a comprehensive treatment of the entire corpus of his thought, could be regarded as serious contributors to the debate, the result would be derisive laughter: it would be all too obvious that this was an attempt to restrict the debate to Wittgensteinians only, and among Wittgensteinians there will surely not be much diversity of opinion as to Wittgenstein's value. But that fact in turn shows that both positive and negative commitment, both the lack of sympathy and the presence of it, are equally likely to shape or misshape an argument. There is as little reason to object a priori to the one as to the other—what matters is the cogency of the argument, not its lineage, and in a healthy climate for debate the former always predominates over the latter.

The tendency to avoid argument by attacking the bona fides of the adversary has, it must be admitted, had its effect on the opposition, which must also be held responsible for the inhibited condition of debate; there is far more grumbling about deconstruction in the corridors of academic institutions than ever finds its way into print. But this is not just an intimidated response to the promise of sharp retaliatory attack. As we shall see in the course of this book, the substance of deconstruction itself is involved, for the dramatic denunciation of the person of common sense and received opinion is an important part of its intellectual orientation. Skeptics know in advance that they are to be cast in that role. The test of whether they have sufficient intellectual sophistication to discuss deconstruction will be that they are able to appreciate so sophisticated a position. Those who question that evaluation ipso facto fail the test and deserve to be regarded with scorn. This attack on the self-confidence of intellectual opponents has probably been assisted by the obscurity of many deconstructive writings; that obscurity makes it difficult to make interpretive statements about them with confidence, and most scholars are loath to commit themselves in print when such confidence is lacking.

My purpose in writing this book, then, is not only to contribute to a debate on deconstruction but to help to create the conditions under which that debate will be possible. It sets out a case against deconstruction. That should neither surprise nor upset anyone. A large number of books set out the case for it; there is nothing wrong with that either. What should be surprising, and upsetting, is that so very little exists on the other side. My book proceeds not by presenting a comprehensive survey of the highways and byways of its subject—that is what a book written by a devotee of a system of thought looks like—but instead by doing what a skeptical account always does and must do, that is, by examining the logic of the central issues and arguments that give the position in question its characteristic quality and that together constitute its major thrust.

The first chapter begins with the question how deconstruction is to be discussed, since this has evidently become an issue in its own right. The next four chapters deal with four major issues in deconstruction. Chapter two begins with that part of Derrida's thought that is widely thought to be the most central to his general outlook: the discussion of language and meaning. Chapters three and four go on to consider deconstructive thinking on critical procedure and on the status of interpretation. Chapter five broadens the inquiry somewhat by considering the view of textual meaning that occurs both in deconstruction and in reader-response criticism. Chapter six returns to the question of the logic of deconstruction but on the basis of the logic that can be abstracted from the arguments considered in chapters two to five, as opposed to the general claims considered in chapter one. Finally, chapter seven looks at deconstruction as a stage in the historical development of literary criticism and theory.

Earlier forms of some of the material included in chapters three and four were first published in *New Literary History* and the *Revue Internationale de Philosophie*. I am grateful to the editors of those journals for permission to reproduce that material again here. I am also indebted to many friends and scholars who have given me helpful comments on earlier drafts of this book, especially Hazard Adams, Trevor Coates, Gerald Graff, William Lillyman, Loisa Nygaard, Siegfried Puknat, Austin Quigley, and Michael Warren.

AGAINST DECONSTRUCTION

CHAPTER ONE

Analysis, Logic, and Argument in Theoretical Discussion

A COMMON ASSUMPTION about theoretical discussion has been that it is a careful, patient, analytical exercise in which precision of formulation, finely drawn distinctions, and all similar marks of cogent, consistent thinking are of the essence. According to this view, theory is the kind of inquiry in which one burrows deeper into ideas and assertions to expose their often hidden ambiguities and implications so that long-standing impasses of argument and understanding can be resolved. Its tone is cool, its manner careful and, above all, analytical. The advent of deconstruction has challenged these assumptions; and since my purpose is to analyze deconstruction itself, it is necessary to devote some time to this matter before we begin.

Scholars who have discussed deconstruction in a critical way have generally elicited the response from its advocates that what they have discussed was not, in fact, deconstruction because any statement or logical analysis of what deconstruction is sins against its nature: it cannot be described and stated as other positions can. To underline this, proponents commonly object to the notion that deconstruction can be thought of as "a theory"; it neither is, nor does it depend on, a theory, they assert. The word *project* is preferred: Derrida's work, and deconstruction, is not a theory but a project. It is not obvious why this change of terminology should make any difference; a project can be characterized just as a theory can, and the resulting characterization can then be examined and analyzed. But the underlying motive in this change of terminology is clear enough: the intent is to make the point that deconstruction cannot be discussed using the tools of reason and logical analysis because it functions in a different way, both requiring and embodying a different logic, a kind of alternative or "other" logic. What are we to make of this stance, and how will it affect our discussion of deconstruction?

A first impulse, when faced with such a question, is to have a look at the case for this "other" logic: what is it? To say that a different kind of logic has been established is to make a large and potentially very exciting claim. To have established it would be a major achievement and an event of the first importance. What does it consist in? How does it work? But its advocates seem more content to use it than to present it explicitly, and direct references to the new logic seem to occur mostly when deconstructive writings are objected to as incoherent or illogical by the standards of the old logic. But this is surely a pity; if an alternative logic is indeed central to deconstruction, one would expect it to be a major focus of discussion and analysis as deconstruction's most central structure and achievement. Why not examine it as well as use it?

To this the answer tends to be that the alternative logic cannot be described and stated as can the old because to describe and state *is* to use the old logic. But we must draw some limits here: granted that standard propositional logic might be inadequate and some other kind might be needed, we still could not allow the claim that a different kind of logic could not be characterized in any way; that would be to exceed the boundaries of all possible logics. A logic must work in some way, and it must be possible to show how it operates and to characterize this operation. If it is claimed that there is a new *kind* of logic that cannot be shown to operate in a way that is identifiable as its own, we should have no reason to know of its existence. It would be like looking at a box that has never been opened and never will be opened and saying that there is something valuable in it. Maybe—but how could we know?

It does not help to reply to this that one can only talk of deconstruction as a performance—the kind of performance embodied in deconstructive writings—for here the same considerations arise that we have already seen in the case of the word *project*. Once again, advocates of deconstruction introduce a term that implies that it is a task or an activity, seemingly in order to avoid the possibility of a characterization that would be available for analysis, but this one, too, fails to achieve its purpose. Just as tasks and projects could not meaningfully be described without reference to their purposes and character, so the mention of an activity could not really make sense unless we also described the kind and function of the activity in question. And once we distinguish the character and intent of the activity from that of other activities, we have again arrived at the statement of the nature and purpose of deconstruction that had previously been resisted. To say this is not to deny that particular discursive statements characterizing a position may be inadequate, especially if they are too brief or simple in their formulation to capture the complexity of an issue or to grasp the nuances of a many-faceted subject. But the remedy in these cases is to object to a brevity that distorts, to demand a fuller formulation that does justice to the matter at hand, and to draw attention to missed subtleties and oversimplifications in order to amend and make those accounts more adequate; none of this has anything to do with the question of whether deconstruction can be characterized, analyzed, or evaluated.

Some attempts have been made to state the nature of the new and different logic, most often in contexts in which an advocate is defending deconstruction against attack. (Though in one case, to be considered below, this statement needs modifying: for in that case the formulation of the "other" logic emerges from an attack, not on a critic, but on an advocate of deconstruction who is denounced as insufficiently devoted to its essential habits of thought.) Of these, one of the most explicit—and in this sense most courageous in its being completely open to scrutiny—is by Barbara Johnson. And, since it takes its cues from Derrida's writings, it can claim his authority. Johnson shows this new logic at work and explains how it transcends the limitations of the old, on two different occasions, referring to two different texts by Derrida.[1] In the first, she cites his *Dissémination*:

[1] Barbara Johnson, "Nothing Fails Like Success," *SCE Reports* 8 (Fall

5

Consider the following passage from Derrida's *Dissémina-tion*: "It is thus not simply false to say that Mallarmé is a Platonist or a Hegelian. But it is above all not true. And vice versa." Instead of a simple either/or structure, deconstruction attempts to elaborate a discourse that says *neither* 'either/or', *nor* 'both/and' nor even 'neither/nor', while at the same time not totally abandoning these logics either.

In the second, she cites a passage from his *Positions* that includes a similar formulation ("Neither/nor, that is, *simulta-neously* either *or*") and comments, "In its deconstruction of the either/or logic of noncontradiction that underlies Western tradition, Derrida's writing attempts to elaborate an 'other' logic." Johnson is certainly abstracting from Derrida's writ-ings in a way that does not distort them, and this is therefore a welcome attempt to explain the alternative logic; she avoids claiming a new logic without offering an explanation and ra-tionale for it. But is it a persuasive diagnosis of anything that could achieve the status of a real alternative logic? Surely, it is not. Consider the matter of the influence on Mallarmé of Plato and Hegel. Presumably, one could pursue a serious and subtle inquiry into the particular ways in which Mallarmé shares common features with, or is indebted to, Plato or Hegel and the ways in which he does not. No one would approach this inquiry thinking that the key question here is whether Mal-larmé is, or is not, identical in all respects with Plato. Those two positions could be discarded immediately. The useful questions have always been, are there sufficient points of con-tact to link the two profitably, and what are they? The more detailed the debate, the more interesting will become the di-agnosis of the relations and possibly contradictions between the two. By the time the inquiry has been pushed to any rea-sonable degree of depth, the question whether Mallarmé is or is not a Platonist will begin to seem rather trite, and anyone who insists on that level of generality will only seem to be in-

---

1980), p. 9, citing Jacques Derrida, *Dissemination*, trans. Barbara Johnson (Chicago, 1981), p. 207; and citing his *Positions*, trans. Alan Bass (Chicago, 1981), p. 43, in the introduction to her translation of *Dissémination*, p. xvii.

terrupting and disrupting something that has gone well beyond this elementary level of analysis. Derrida's statement that it is neither true nor false to say that Mallarmé is a Platonist works only on that level of generality and is therefore surely devoid of substantial content. To do no more than contemplate the extremes of Mallarmé's being either totally Platonist or not in any way Platonist adds nothing to the inquiry beyond two simple and equally unpromising positions and the implication (for is anything else implied here?) that the truth is somewhere between them. But where else could it be?

The key to what is really being done here is surely in the closing "vice versa"; it is a redundancy whose function is to give an impression of a daring leap from one position to another and back again. But if *all* the positions concerned are equally uninteresting, what has this achieved? To this question, there appears to be only one possible answer: what is gained is not sophistication of logic but instead the *appearance* of sophistication and complexity. Perhaps the notion of performance is appropriate here, but it seems in this example to be a performance that uses rhetorical devices to create the illusion of sophisticated analysis where none really exists. In *any* argument whether and to what degree X is A or B (for example, whether interpretation is objective or subjective and to what degree one or the other; or to what degree Mallarmé is a Platonist or not) it would be very easy for anyone to say that X is A, it is B, it is neither, and it is both and vice versa, for good measure. My point is that one would not need to be informed about the issues to say as much and, correspondingly, that one has not made a substantial assertion about the issues having said as much. This kind of rhetoric does not advance serious thought or inquiry but gives an impression of profundity and complexity without the effort and skill that would be required to make a substantial contribution to the understanding of the matter under discussion.

But more importantly still, the character of the performance is most unoriginal: for the rhetorical device used here is simply the standard formula of many branches of religious mysticism. As a leading authority on mysticism writes in a standard introductory essay, "Mystical experience permits complementary and apparently contradictory modes of expression. . . . This is because the reality affirmed contains its own opposite."[2] Derrida and Johnson have, then, seized on an ancient rhetorical device for their new, "other" logic, but the mere application of this standard mystical formula to a question of literary influences does nothing to advance discussion of that question.

Johnson's attempt to establish the character of deconstructive logic is, it must be said, a brave attempt to deal with this matter in direct, intelligible terms; but that is why its failure is discouraging. Indeed, the result of her effort is not to showcase an example of the new logic, as she intends, but instead to expose a weakness of deconstruction—the seeming attraction to rhetorical brilliance per se. And this failed attempt to expound a new logic of deconstruction is discouraging in still another way. If Johnson's attempt had been met with a negative response from most other scholars who work within the deconstructive mode, its failure could be thought of as hers alone; but, to the contrary, it met with a predominantly favorable response.[3]

---

[2] Sisirkumar Ghose, *Encyclopaedia Britannica*, 15th ed., s.v. "Mysticism," Macropedia: 12, 786–93. Similar formulas, taken from many different branches of mysticism, both Christian and non-Christian, occur throughout Ghose's introductory survey, e.g.: "What is below is like what is above, what is above is like what is below"; "the mystic is both in and out of time"; etc. "The rhetoric of mysticism," we are told, "is largely one of symbols and paradoxes." Much like deconstruction.

[3] Johnson's paper "Nothing Fails Like Success" was in fact the showpiece of the session entitled "Deconstructive Criticism: Directions" of the Society for Critical Exchange at the 1980 meeting of the Modern Language Association of America, to which all other participants were invited to respond. Jerry Aline Flieger ("The Art of Being Taken by Surprise," *SCE Reports* 8, Fall 1980), one of a number who received Johnson's paper favorably, asserted that the "old" logic that deconstruction replaced was the logic of "binary oppositions," i.e., contrasts of opposing terms. But in an amusing contradiction immediately following this, she decided that the way to "pin down the 'unclear' logic of deconstruction" was to proceed by distinguishing it from traditional logic: "the clearest distinction between traditionalist and deconstructive logic resides in . . ." (p. 57). In other words, binary logic is needed to characterize

Aside from this one specific attempt to characterize the "other" logic, the claims made for it are mostly of an extremely general character, but this generality brings with it a weakness of a different kind. When, for example, it is claimed that Derrida must be judged and evaluated by different logical standards, standards uniquely appropriate to him, there is no explanation of just what those standards are and how they are to be justified; without some kind of explanation, this claim cannot be granted. If it were allowed to stand, no debate on or evaluation of differing viewpoints would be possible; theory would degenerate into a series of solipsistic monologues without any points of contact between them. But this claim in any case regularly breaks down as advocates abandon it in order to discuss Derrida in relation to other thinkers and thus use terms and procedures to discuss him that drop the claim for a separate linguistic and logical world.

Perhaps the most common claim of all here is simply the most general of all: that logic, reason, and analysis are insufficient to discuss Derrida. But this is so general that it places Derrida in a much larger, not smaller, group and so effectively withdraws any claim for a unique status for him. For this is a claim made with great regularity throughout human history; attacks on rational thought have occurred with regularity by mystics, visionaries, and others who were similarly impatient with the constraints of reason. Thus Derrida, far from being unique, would now be seen as just another among many in this tradition of thought; but once again it is not at all clear that he and his followers are really consistent in this claim, because, as we shall see, they also tend to abandon it when discussing specific issues.

Jonathan Culler's expositions of deconstruction frequently provoke a statement of this generalized claim for an exemption from logic and rational analysis. Mas'd Zavarzadeh, for example, attacks Culler for his "deeply rooted conservatism,

---

deconstructive logic. This example, like many others, leads to the thought that these claims for an "other" logic have often been too lightly made without being adequately thought through.

in which his mediations tame radical new ideas," and for "his unproblematic prose and the clarity of his presentation, which are the conceptual tools of conservatism."[4] The assumption here is evidently that rational analysis is inherently an inappropriate and unfair means of approaching deconstruction. Similarly, Steven Rendall has recently written that "Culler's measured, systematic and reassuring exposition risks exposing him to the charge that he is contributing to the recuperation and revitalization of deconstruction by the American critical establishment. I do not think the charge can be summarily dismissed."[5] And Rendall points to the issue of "distortions" and "simplifications" in Culler's exposition, not as a specific matter of the particular points Culler has *misstated* when he could and should have stated them properly (for no examples are given), but rather as a general issue of distortion and simplification that *must* be present whenever any clear and rational exposition occurs.

It is important to remember that this is no longer, as was the case with Johnson, an attempt to demonstrate a specific alternative logic for deconstruction but instead a general attack on clear, systematic argument. And since no specific instances are used to show how a clear, rational exposition distorts a specific issue, so that we can see how the general point works in specific terms, the claim remains a vague one, lacking any demonstration of how and why it is justified.

While the attitudes we have been considering may seem to borrow the traditional attitudes of mysticism and other forms of irrationalism, it must be noted that most other aspects of what deconstructionists do and say are quite inconsistent with

---

[4] Mas'd Zavarzadeh, review of Jonathan Culler's *The Pursuit of Signs* (Ithaca, 1981), in *Journal of Aesthetics and Art Criticism* 40 (1982), pp. 329–33.

[5] Steven Rendall, review of Jonathan Culler's *On Deconstruction: Theory of Criticism after Structuralism* (Ithaca, 1982), in *Comparative Literature* 36 (1984), pp. 263–68. Frank Lentricchia, too, hints that Culler softens the impact of modern French thought and has made "structuralism safe for us" (*After the New Criticism*, Chicago, 1980, pp. 104–105). Since devotees of recent French thought tend to hail it as essentially disturbing, disorienting, and revolutionary, this is of course a very damning criticism: on this view, the *major* thrust is lost in Culler's exposition.

those traditional positions. For the very instruments of rational thinking are words and arguments, and deconstruction is very verbal and very argumentative.

Take, for example, Joseph Riddel's attempt to defend deconstruction against Gerald Graff's criticisms: "Certainly the reactionaries, and Graff's work is a reductive example, contain the question by turning what they understand of deconstruction—having turned it first into a 'buzz' word—into a series of summary ontological statements and then denouncing those statements as illogical."[6] Riddel's objection is to Graff's first characterizing deconstruction and then leveling objections against that characterization. But note the uncertainty in Riddel's position: the specific objections he makes sin against his general position. He should have stopped at objecting to *any* summary characterization of deconstruction. But when he accuses Graff of using "buzz" words, he is of course accusing him not of being logical (the only consistent objection) but instead of being illogical, of using the tools of rational discourse *badly*. Similarly, he accuses Graff of making a *reductive* summary of deconstruction—i.e., of summarizing deconstruction in an inaccurate, distorting way. One cannot have it both ways: either Graff's discussion sins against deconstruction by logically *faulty* exposition (using "buzz" words, reductive distortions) or it sins by using description and analysis at all. Not both. To charge that a statement of someone's position is reductive is to make a *logical* objection, which commits the maker of that charge to *showing how a more adequate formulation was necessary*. But this charge cannot be allied with a general attack on *any* attempt to state and describe a position. One can, in fact, abstract from Riddel's com-

[6] Joseph N. Riddel, "What Is Deconstruction, and Why Are They Writing All Those Graff-ic Things About It?" *SCE Reports* 8 (Fall 1980), p. 21. Doubtless, Graff's criticisms of deconstruction have been the most forceful and substantial to date. See especially his "Deconstruction as Dogma, or, 'Come Back to the Raft Ag'in, Strether Honey!' " *Georgia Review* 34 (1980), pp. 404–21; "Culler and Deconstruction," *London Review of Books* (3–16 September 1981); and "The Pseudo Politics of Interpretation," *Critical Inquiry* 9 (1983), pp. 597–610.

ments *two* possible responses to arguments objecting to deconstruction: the first would be to charge reductiveness and show how the characterization offered by an opponent is faulty or inadequate; the second would be to claim that any rational statement and discussion is out of the question for deconstruction, and stop there. A charge of inaccuracy belongs to the first mode, and it presupposes a possible correction of the inaccuracy. Clearly, this kind of advocate of deconstruction wants things both ways: he wants to claim reductiveness and inaccuracy (the first mode) but then avoids the *specific* argument required in that mode by going over to the second. Even more serious, however, is the fact that the second mode, in addition to disallowing any allegations of inaccuracy or inadequacy in critical discussions of deconstruction, would prohibit any characterizations of deconstruction by its proponents, too. But proponents are certainly unwilling to accept any restriction on their own ability to characterize and evaluate deconstruction.

When discussing deconstruction amongst themselves (and therefore not under attack from the outside) deconstructionists do not hesitate to state a position or to talk of correct and incorrect versions of that position, often asking directly whether a particular formulation is correct. J. Hillis Miller, for example, in reviewing his fellow deconstructionist Joseph Riddel's book *The Inverted Bell*, asks the perfectly old-fashioned question, "First, there is the question of Riddel's reading of Heidegger and Derrida. Has he got them right?"[7] Rodolphe Gasché even goes so far as to say that all American advocates of deconstruction are guilty of misunderstanding it.[8]

[7] J. Hillis Miller, "Deconstructing the Deconstructors," review of *The Inverted Bell: Modernism and the Counterpoetics of William Carlos Williams*, by Joseph N. Riddel, *Diacritics* 5 (1975), pp. 26–31.

[8] Rodolphe Gasché, "Deconstruction as Criticism," *Glyph* 6 (1979), pp. 177–215. Similar opinions among those who concern themselves with Derrida's work are, in fact, quite common; see, for example, Lentricchia, p. 178: "much of what is claimed in Derrida's name bears only the most tenuous relationship to what in fact he has been writing"; and William V. Spanos, "Retrieving Heidegger's De-Struction: A Response to Barbara Johnson," *SCE Reports* 8 (Fall 1980), p. 30.

Advocates generally see no problem, then, in claiming to characterize deconstruction *correctly* in opposition to an incorrect characterization by other advocates. And they are *specific*—that is, they state the error, refer to the mischaracterized version, and offer the version they believe to be more adequate; all of which tends to throw doubt on the seriousness of the claim that deconstruction is a position that cannot be stated and that any attempt to state it must of necessity be reductive and distorting. When deconstruction is not under attack, we find the usual business of statement, objection, and restatement being carried forward with specific arguments being countered by others. The attempt to veto rational argument is encountered most when the wolf is at the door.

But what of Derrida himself on this point? During his much-publicized dispute with John Searle,[9] Derrida clearly conceded the point at issue. Believing that Searle's exposition of his position had been unfair to him, Derrida could not resist saying, at several points in his reply, that Searle had misunderstood him and misstated his views, even adding at one point that what he, Derrida, had meant should have been clear enough and obvious to Searle. This is indeed a very far cry from the claim that Derrida's essential position cannot be stated as others can[10] (or that a reader should not try to grasp

[9] This exchange began with Derrida's essay "Signature, Event, Context," *Glyph* 1 (1977), pp. 172–97, to which Searle replied with "Reiterating the Differences: A Reply to Derrida," *Glyph* 1 (1977), pp. 198–208. Derrida's riposte was "Limited, Inc. abc," *Glyph* 2 (1977), pp. 162–254. In an unguarded moment, Frank Lentricchia also accuses "the Yale group" of misconstruing Derrida's work by "ignoring . . . an important part of its author's intention" (*After the New Criticism*, Chicago, 1980, p. 170), a formulation at odds with Derrida's objection to the notion that an author's intention controls the meaning of his text, which again raises doubt about the depth of the commitment to this idea.

[10] It also contradicts other important deconstructive positions that will be discussed in later chapters, i.e., that the original/originary meaning is not a controlling factor in textual interpretation; that all interpretations are misinterpretations; that since the free play of signs is infinite, a text has no clear meaning; etc. Derrida goes counter to all of these positions by insisting that *his* intention is controlling, that it *is* the meaning of his text, that Searle *could* have interpreted it correctly, and that his meaning should have been *clear*.

the author's intent!). Derrida thus abandons this position, just as others do, when he feels the need to replace a misstatement of his view with an adequate statement of it.

And so the claim that deconstruction is a special case, not to be judged or discussed by rational argument and ordinary logic, is a claim that is neither explicated nor really consistently believed and acted upon by those who make it. Where does this leave us? In the chapters that follow, I shall discuss and evaluate some central aspects of deconstruction. In pursuing this discussion I make the following assumptions, which seem to me fundamental ones that are not seriously challenged by any of the claims made for deconstruction as a special case:

1. Derrida and others who follow him make pronouncements and arguments that—whether one calls them theories or not and whatever the kind of logic that is claimed as their basis—can be discussed, examined, scrutinized, and analyzed with a view to reaching a judgment and conclusion as to whether they are useful or pointless, cogent or incoherent, compelling or unconvincing, original or derivative, just as is the case anywhere and at any time.

Michael Fischer (*Does Deconstruction Make Any Difference?* Bloomington, 1985, pp. 40–41) notes that some of Derrida's followers are embarrassed by the obvious inconsistency between Derrida's general position and his "aggrieved tone" as he accuses Searle of having misunderstood him, and they try to deal with the problem by claiming that Derrida is being ironic. Fischer is doubtless correct in insisting that Derrida's anger and the reason for it are nonetheless unmistakable, that his ironic disclaimers never erase the accusations that they follow, and that the character of those accusations undermines the position he is defending. To this one could add that those same followers generally have also done exactly what embarrassed them when they saw Derrida doing it (i.e., they too routinely accuse Searle of misunderstanding, missing the point of, and misstating Derrida's position) and that the extraordinary length of Derrida's reply (nearly a hundred pages, ten times the length of Searle's piece, and half of many a book in length!) is not consistent with irony's light touch. It is, rather, indicative of considerable seriousness of purpose and is barely conceivable except on the hypothesis that Derrida was smarting under what he had felt to be some damaging blows.

2. When any new view appears and arouses interest among a fairly broad group of observers, it is in everyone's interest to see it discussed widely, by insiders and admirers just as much as by outsiders and critics.

If I feel the need to state such simple assumptions, it is because most of the previous discussion of this chapter essentially concerned attempts to evade them. The half-hearted claim of a different logic, usually without an attempt to meet the challenge of developing and justifying so grand an idea; the weakness of the few, sketchy attempts to say what this new logic might be; the degeneration of this idea into a general rejection of reason, argument, and logic; the reluctance to allow that deconstruction can be characterized and that characterization subjected to evaluation; the fact of this reluctance generally appearing when deconstruction is under attack and its disappearance in other, less threatening contexts—all of this, taken together, seems more indicative of an exaggerated anxiety about counterarguments than of genuine intellectual conviction. And it seems, indeed, to be an extension of the reflex that I mentioned in my preface, namely, the habit of dealing with criticism not by meeting the specific arguments that have been made but by identifying the critic as hostile and not competent to make criticisms,[11] except that here emphasis shifts to the claim that criticisms by non-deconstructionists can never be deconstructive enough in their logic to be taken seriously.

Some attacks on deconstruction may well be reductive and distorting, and it is not in principle inconceivable that deconstruction could require some readjustment in the way in which we analyze and evaluate ideas. The point, however, is not that these assertions may not be true but that in the absence of any more specific explanation and demonstration they are incomplete and, until completed, lacking in force.

[11] This has been noted by, e.g., Graff, "Culler and Deconstruction," and Frederick Crews, in his recent "In the Big House of Theory," *New York Review of Books* (29 May 1986).

There is something very odd about a situation in which a major intellectual development is said to have arrived, but at the same time it is also said that one should not try to state what it is or proceed with analyzing and evaluating it. The more important the new idea, the more one would expect the ordinary process of questioning and redefinition to be necessary. Any new argument is likely to contain an occasional confused and ambiguous concept, for example, or argument that fails through relying on mutually exclusive senses of the same word. Part of the function of adverse criticism is to root out these flaws.[12]

In spite of all that is said of the impossibility of stating what deconstruction is, I doubt there will be any real disagreement that the four themes that I discuss in the following chapters are indeed major issues within deconstruction. The dangers of inaccurate statement can never be completely avoided, and that is particularly the case when, as in Derrida's case, we are dealing with a body of writings that are often obscure—deliberately so, if we are to believe his admirers.[13] For this reason I

[12] It is worth noting that there is a long-standing tradition of claiming immunity from logical scrutiny in criticism that predates deconstruction; of this, and its relation to this latest example of that claim, more below in chapter seven.

[13] This obscurity itself is sometimes adduced as the reason why one should not try to state deconstruction's positions and arguments in direct, comprehensible terms in order to discuss them: thus difficulty and obscurity are simply equated with complexity and profundity. Since most of our experience is decidedly to the contrary—that is, texts that are difficult and obscure are most usually confused and poorly thought out—this can never be an automatic assumption; it needs to be demonstrated anew in each case claimed to be an exception to the general rule. It cannot be assumed without argument, then, that Derrida's obscure style precludes any possibility of his ideas being infected with confusions and faulty inferences; obscurity, far from insuring against this, as a general rule makes it more, not less, likely. Derrida, however, explicitly appeals to his own obscurity as a defense in the exchange with Searle cited above. After Searle had pointed to some logical errors in his work, Derrida replied that the essay in question was a *difficult* work, chiding Searle for not recognizing this. But we usually assume that, if an author's difficult and obscure style is admitted by that author to have been the source of a reader's misunderstanding him, the reader might be entitled to chide the author and not vice versa. The necessity of an obscure style is sometimes said to

have, in what follows, attempted to make statements by Derrida himself, and by English speaking deconstructionists generally acknowledged as leading exponents, the basis of my discussion. Meanwhile, the subject of a specifically deconstructive logic is one to which I shall return in chapter six, but with a different perspective. There the subject of discussion will no longer be the general claims made for a new deconstructive logic but, instead, the typical logic of deconstructive arguments that can be abstracted from its actual practice.

---

follow from deconstruction's viewpoint on language and meaning; this point takes us directly to the next chapter, where that view is discussed.

CHAPTER TWO

Deconstruction and the Nature of Language

IN CONTEMPORARY WRITINGS on the theory of criticism, Derrida's position is a commanding one, so much so that there is a growing tendency to assume that an interest in theory of criticism automatically means an interest in the work of Derrida. Enthusiasm for recent developments is very likely to consist in a welcoming of the liberating influence of deconstruction, and thus any assessment of the achievements and limitations of the present state of this field would have to concern itself centrally with Derrida. The most influential and central aspect of Derrida's thought in this regard, meanwhile, has been his treatment of language and meaning. We must begin by looking at what is most characteristic in those ideas and evaluating their importance and cogency.

In his most widely read work, *Of Grammatology*,[1] Derrida begins with an argument concerning the relationship between speech and writing. The argument focuses on the question of the priority of one over the other and what that priority means for language in general and meaning in particular. He first observes that the Western tradition has regarded writing as inferior to speech and as a mere representation of speech that was thus at one stage removed from the essence of language. He argues that the reverse should be the case: "I shall try to show later that there is no linguistic sign before writing,"[2] and "the

[1] Jacques Derrida, *Of Grammatology*, trans. Gayatri Chakravorty Spivak (Baltimore, 1976). I have cited the English version of the published translations of Derrida throughout this book but in each case have checked them against the original French to make sure that they do not introduce changes of emphasis that would have any significant bearing on the course of my argument. Responsibility for any distortion of the issues discussed here because of the translation is thus also my responsibility, not solely that of the translator.

[2] Ibid., p. 14.

concept of writing exceeds and comprehends that of language."[3] The failure to accord writing this importance and priority over speech is due to "the *ethnocentrism* which, everywhere and always, had controlled the concept of writing."[4] Far from being a system invented to record the already existing phenomenon of language, then, writing is more central to language than speech itself. "Far from being speech's shadow," writes Derrida's expositor Terence Hawkes, "writing captures language's essence."[5] Ferdinand de Saussure is specifically identified as a leading purveyor of this ethnocentrism: "The contamination by writing, the fact or the threat of it, are denounced in the accents of the moralist or preacher by the linguist from Geneva."[6]

Before assessing this first step in Derrida's argument, it is as well to note that Derrida later modifies this account considerably, yet without making the point any less important for his further argument; but it will help to understand the reason for the modification if we set out immediately some serious problems in what he has said so far. There are some obvious logical objections to consider, as well as one matter of historical fact on which Derrida is clearly wrong. I will take up the historical matter first.

Derrida's account of the Western tradition—specifically, of its ethnocentrism and Saussure's participating in that ethnocentrism—reverses the historical situation and constitutes a major misunderstanding. Far from being a purveyor of the traditional ethnocentrism, Saussure opposed the ethnocentrism of Western linguists who had always paid too much attention to the texts and manuscripts of written language, to the detriment of speech. This traditional emphasis on written texts automatically involved a limited, ethnocentric perspective on language, since it restricted study to those cultures and languages with long written traditions, i.e., largely their own Western cultures; historical philologists, his main target of at-

[3] Ibid., p. 8.
[4] Ibid., p. 3.
[5] Terence Hawkes, *Structuralism and Semiotics* (Berkeley and Los Angeles, 1977), p. 148.
[6] Derrida, *Of Grammatology*, p. 34.

tack, had especially restricted themselves to written sources and thus were largely ethnocentrically concerned with their own corner of the world. Saussure's importance was to turn linguistics away from this prevailing *ethnocentric concern with the written* and toward the spoken languages of that part of the world outside the Western tradition. And so, it is a mistake to say (1) that Western tradition had been antiwriting and prospeech prior to Saussure, (2) that Saussure's thrust was ethnocentric rather than a corrective of a pervasive ethnocentrism, and (3) that Saussure is a purveyor of this Western tradition rather than one who turns decisively against it.[7] In all three issues, Derrida states Saussure's role in a way that is the reverse of what it actually was.

This is a discouraging beginning, for deconstruction has much at stake in this diagnosis of an ethnocentrism and its being overcome. It is somewhat characteristic of deconstructive arguments that they claim to seize on unexamined assumptions of all kinds—ethnocentrism being one—in order to explode and transcend them, hoping to alter and enlarge our consciousness of the issues concerned. But in this case, our consciousness of the issues is merely distorted, for the ethnocentrism is misdiagnosed. Indeed, it is easier to see in Derrida's position here, not a corrective to ethnocentrism, but instead a determined *reassertion* of the ethnocentrism that Saussure sought to correct and transcend, for he is thoroughly commit-

---

[7] John Searle, in his "The Word Turned Upside Down," a review of Jonathan Culler's *On Deconstruction* (*New York Review of Books* 30, 27 October 1983, pp. 73–79), also argues against Derrida's diagnosis of the Western tradition here, using the history of philosophical thought for his examples rather than the misconceptions about Saussure's position in the history of linguistics that I have used. Note, however, how very little it takes to defeat Derrida's point once Derrida has committed himself, as he does, to the view that "*everywhere* and *always*" (my italics) this ethnocentrism has prevailed. Both Searle and I argue, in effect, that the majority viewpoint in different areas of thought has been the other way round, but Derrida's "everywhere and always" is so sweeping and categorical that *one* example would suffice to defeat it. And while this is, in a way, just one example of an extreme of formulation introduced very commonly into deconstructive arguments by the use of the words *always* and *everywhere*, in this case it is, as we shall see below, an essential part of Derrida's argument rather than an incautiously extreme formulation of it.

ted to the primacy of the written word—the "bookishness"—
that is so typical of the Western intellectual tradition.[8]

More important still are the obvious logical problems involved in asserting that writing is prior to speech. Here we
must deal with a strange fact: these objections are so very obvious that they seem barely to need stating, and yet they are
almost never alluded to in the voluminous literature on deconstruction. It is as if there were a belief abroad that any objections so simple as these must be beneath the level of sophistication required to make a contribution to this debate:

1. Speech quite clearly existed long before the *invention* of
writing.
2. There still exist in the world languages that are spoken
but not written, but none that are written without being
spoken.
3. There are large numbers of individuals who speak
without writing, but none who write without speaking
(except when their physical capacity to produce speech is
deficient).
4. There are many different forms of writing, but linguists
of all persuasions agree that *no* form of writing in general
use is adequate to record all that there is in language;
intonation, stress, pitch, and other communicative features
are not adequately dealt with even in the best writing
systems. All writing systems are *in principle* only attempts
to represent languages that *must* in varying degrees be
incomplete.

Given the fact that most of this is obvious, what is Derrida's
argument trying to do, and why does he not explain the fact
that (presumably, in his view) none of these points are relevant
to it? Most expositors of Derrida's thought pass over this mat-

---

[8] Derrida's view of Saussure as a traditionalist, rather than as the revolutionary figure in the history of linguistic study in Europe that he really was,
has been accepted with surprising and saddening swiftness by many of his
expositors—not a very hopeful indicator of their knowledge of the history of
linguistics. Frank Lentricchia, for example, speaks easily and unquestioningly
of Saussure's "traditionalist ploy" (*After the New Criticism*, Chicago, 1980,
p. 175).

ter in silence. Perhaps the explanation for this is indeed a feeling that the argument would drop below the required level of complexity if it dealt with them. But this would be a very dangerous attitude; the objections may be obvious, but that does not mean that it is equally obvious how they can be answered. No argument can avoid degenerating into unreality if the need to deal with obvious counterarguments is not keenly felt. And, indeed, as we shall see, the further development of this issue both in Derrida and his expositors shows quite clearly that they *do* find these problems serious and oppressive ones and that they have great difficulty in handling them.

Culler is one of very few to face the issue squarely, stating some of the possible objections, then giving an answer:

> In defense of this ranking [i.e., the traditional ranking of speech above writing] one may cite the fact that children learn to speak before they learn to write or that millions of people, even entire cultures, have speech without writing; but when such facts are adduced they are taken to demonstrate not just a factual or logical priority of speech to writing but a more portentous general and comprehensive priority. Speech is seen as in direct contact with meaning.[9]

But this answer only makes matters very much worse, for in attempting to deal with an objection, Culler manages to put his finger on the tremendous force of the objection and then fails to answer it. He has to concede that what is being denied by Derrida's argument is neither temporal (factual) priority nor logical priority; it is only, apparently, "a more portentous general and comprehensive priority." But what could this vague notion possibly mean? How could a general priority—speech taking general precedence over writing—mean anything besides temporal or logical priority? (Culler's further explanation of this goes into issues that do not relate to the issue of the priority of the two at all; but to this we shall return.)

[9] Culler was perhaps compelled to deal with these problems by the fact that in 1976 his *Structuralist Poetics* (Ithaca, 1976, p. 133) was openly skeptical on this matter of Derrida's view of the priority of writing over speech, while by 1983 he had become an advocate of it. The passage cited is from his *On Deconstruction* (Ithaca, 1982), p. 100.

Derrida's own extension of his argument shows equally clearly that the obvious objections set out above are too difficult to overcome. For the real effect of this extension is a withdrawal from the position he first enunciated—but a covert, unacknowledged withdrawal:

> If "writing" signifies inscription and especially the durable institution of a sign (and that is the only irreducible kernel of the concept of writing), writing in general covers the entire field of linguistic signs. In that field a certain sort of instituted signifiers may then appear, "graphic" in the narrow and derivative sense of the word, ordered by a certain relationship with other instituted—hence "written," even if they are "phonic"—signifiers. The very idea of institution—hence of the arbitrariness of the sign—is unthinkable before the possibility of writing and outside its horizon.[10]

There are many holes in this argument; let us first look at its lesser problems before considering the one that is most serious and most indicative of the general untenability of Derrida's argument.

First of all, Derrida's assertion that the idea of the institution of signs (that is, the arising of language through a set of signs becoming institutionalized as a system employed in a community of speakers) is unthinkable before the *possibility* of writing achieves nothing whatever. To assert that as soon as speech arises, writing it down is possible, might *at best* be to argue for the *equal* status of speech and writing. The argument for this equal status might then continue that speech is not prior to writing because at the very moment speech exists, writing *could* exist. But that is *not* support for Derrida's claim that writing is prior to speech. And, in fact, even the argument here for equal status fails. Even in admitting that speech cannot exist until writing is *possible*, Derrida is conceding the *logical* priority of speech, since it is speech's *existence* that makes writing *possible*.

The second point is that Derrida's attempt to shift the meaning of the word *writing* by saying that the "only irreduc-

[10] *Of Grammatology*, p. 44.

ible kernel of the concept of writing" is the "durable institution of a sign" also fails. He is plainly wrong as to the "irreducible" kernel of the idea of writing. What is irreducibly essential to the idea of writing is the *visual* recording of the sign. Since the advent of the tape recorder, signs both visual (writing) and audible (speech) can be durable. Derrida's omission of the one truly distinctive and irreducible kernel element of the word *writing* means that he misstates the core meaning of the word, and only this key omission allows him to proceed as he does to claim that writing includes speech. One last point here: the appeal to an "irreducible kernel" of meaning in any term is surely completely inconsistent with the further course of Derrida's ideas on language and meaning, as we shall see; in other words, Derrida, given where he wants to go next, is not in a position to advance an argument that appeals to an irreducible kernel of *anything*. He will soon rule out the possibility of any central, essential meaning for a word.

The major objection to this stage of Derrida's argument, however, lies in its being an example of a very well known logical mistake. We begin with three terms: language, speech, and writing. The first contains the second and third. The question is now which of these last two has priority. Derrida is attempting to prove that the third has priority over the second, in the face of some obvious arguments to the contrary. To do so, he replaces our first triad of terms (language, speech, writing) with a different triad: writing, phonic, graphic. He substitutes the second triad for the first, and now writing has precedence over everything.

It is not difficult to see what is wrong with this procedure. First of all, the nature of the phenomenon concerned has *not* been changed. If we decide arbitrarily to call language "writing," speech "phonic," and writing "graphic," we have not changed the relation of the three entities: what we ordinarily call "language" still stands in the same relationship to speech and writing whether we use these three names or the other three. Second, this procedure does, of course, involve a misuse of English. Language does *not* mean writing, and if we use "writing" to substitute for "language" we have misspoken.

This structure of argument is, in effect, an admission of failure. It is always possible to make any assertion true by redefining terms until the assertion is true by definition, regardless of facts; and it is a logical commonplace that an argument that can only proceed in this way achieves nothing.[11] If an argument is made that A does not have priority over B, where all the facts suggest the reverse, the last resort will be to change the meaning of term A so that it is redefined as falling under category B. That makes the argument true only at the cost of making it meaningless. For at the outset, the argument was about the relation of the two admittedly distinguishable entities, and it must proceed by continuing to deal with those things that distinguish them. Derrida, by contrast, starts with and *insists on* the distinction speech/writing but is only able to prove his point by abandoning the distinction and insisting that they are both the same, that is, by redefining one half of the distinction to cover both. But it is clear that his redefined "writing" (*not* the word with the meaning we all use) is not employed anywhere else in his argument—its sole use is to save his thesis at this particular point. Elsewhere, both before and after this stage of his argument, "writing" really means "writing."[12]

[11] See, for example, John Searle's related diagnosis in his review of Culler's *On Deconstruction.*

[12] That (contrary to what is often claimed by his followers) Derrida continues to use the word *writing* in its normal sense, even after his virtual redefinition of it, can easily be seen in the later parts of his *Of Grammatology,* for example, those in which he elaborates his ideas through a discussion of Rousseau's ideas on language: "In the *Confessions,* when Jean-Jacques tries to explain how he became a writer, he describes the passage to writing as the restoration, by a certain absence and by a sort of calculated effacement, of presence disappointed" (p. 142). Derrida's choosing to develop his own ideas on language through an extensive critique of those of Rousseau must remain something of a puzzle; among linguistic theorists, Rousseau's ideas scarcely count as a serious contribution to the field, and much of what Rousseau has to say would have to count as dismissably crackpot taken in the context of modern linguistic theory. Moreover, Derrida actually discusses, in all seriousness, precisely those aspects of Rousseau's views that are most obviously so, e.g., "The Languages of the North are 'clear because of the power of words'; in the languages of the South, 'the meaning is only half in the words, all the force is in the accents' " or " 'Our tongues are better suited to writing than speaking . . . Oriental tongues, on the other hand, lose their life and warmth

Derrida's argument that writing is prior to speech is, then, a failure; but there is a very strange aspect of it that we have not yet touched upon. Throughout, he uses oddly moralistic terms to describe the opposing view. He speaks of the "debasement of writing, and its *repression* . . . ," of the "signs of liberation all over the world," of writing being "enslaved," of its being "feared and subversive." These seem strangely inappropriate moral terms for a discussion of writing. In some contexts perhaps, we might use the word fear in connection with writing. But those contexts would be the restricted ones of writer's block, dyslexia, or perhaps a five-year-old's learning anxiety. We might use the word *subversive* in connection with writing in the context of a dictator's illiterate population. But Derrida's context is not these: it is an argument about the logical priority of speech and writing. In *this* context, does it really make sense to say that anyone has ever *feared* writing? Still less that *most of us* fear writing? Or that we find writing subversive? Or that we enslave it? I doubt that it would ever be intelligent to say that writing is, generally, repressed—what could that possibly mean? All over the world, *enormous* quantities of writing are turned out every day: books, newspapers, journals, reports, pamphlets, advertisements, magazines, etc. In the face of this truly prodigious production and consumption of writing, can we possibly think of it as repressed? And the announcement of "signs of liberation all over the world"—what can this possibly refer to? It sounds like a call to arms, a crusade—but *what* crusade? Does it really exist?

These dramatic, moralistic terms might be regarded as merely exuberant metaphors were it not for two facts. First, it will be remembered that it was Derrida who denounced Saussure for this trait: "The contamination by writing . . . [is] *denounced in the accents of the moralist or preacher* by the linguist from Geneva" (emphasis mine). It is surely odd that Derrida objects to the much milder text of Saussure when his own text is moralistic in tone to an extravagant degree. Sec-

---

when they are written' " (*Of Grammatology*, p. 226). One is left to wonder, why should such dated and now surely dismissable opinions be worth the considerable space Derrida devotes to their critique? Why would he not wish to develop his notions on language through a critique of modern thought?

ond, the crusading tone appears to be so predominant that it must be considered an important aspect of Derrida's text. Its dramatic quality is quite evidently a strong part of the appeal to his followers;[13] he, and they, really do feel the exhilaration of liberating writing from an enslaved, repressed condition, however oddly these notions contrast with the extraordinarily healthy current condition of writing and however much they seem out of place in a discussion of the logical priority of speech and language. But what really makes this sense of moral urgency and drama strangest of all is that, when Derrida's next step is looked at closely, this entire fallacious argument about the priority of speech and language is found to be unnecessary for the main course of his thought: it could be dropped without loss.

Derrida himself never abandons his crusade against the reductive attitude to writing and continues to insist that it is "part and parcel of phonologism and logocentrism."[14] But of the two, logocentrism is his main target. An indication of the further direction of his thinking is seen in the remark that the "structural possibility of being weaned from the referent or from the signified (hence from communication and from its context) seems to me to make every mark, including those which are oral, a grapheme in general."[15] Once again, that part of this statement that concerns the relation of speech to writing does not work. The fact that a word can be cited and used independent of communication and context has nothing to do with the issue of speech versus writing, for it can happen equally in both; and Derrida's argument that because any word can be cited orally, all words must be graphemes (i.e., written) clearly fails. The fact that citation can be done orally proves exactly the reverse, that citation is *not* necessarily written. But here we see why Derrida is so concerned with this mistaken idea: his real aim is to make an argument about the

---

[13] To take one prominent example, Christopher Norris's summary of this aspect of Derrida's argument (in his *Deconstruction: Theory and Practice*, London and New York, 1982, pp. 27–31) is heavily dependent on these same moralistic terms and their high drama.

[14] Jacques Derrida, *Positions*, trans. Alan Bass (Chicago, 1981), p. 24.

[15] Jacques Derrida, "Signature, Event, Context," *Glyph* 1 (1977), p. 183.

relation between language and its referent, and his concern with the priority of writing and speech derives from his wishing to use it as support in his major argument. This is evidently because he wants to use what he thinks to be the characteristic quality of writing as the essential character of language for the purposes of his argument about the relation of language to reality.

It would have been possible to achieve this purpose without making the impossible claim that writing is prior to speech. Derrida's expositor, Culler, puts his point far more defensibly than Derrida himself when he says, "writing . . . turns out to be the best illustration of the nature of linguistic units."[16] And indeed the further course of Derrida's argument involves the point that a focus on speech will predispose us to a certain erroneous view of meaning—speech *seems* to be immediately linked to meaning in an illusory way. It would be quite sufficient, then, for him to argue that a certain fundamental error in linguistic theory arises from an illusion created more readily by the typical situation of speech but that this error is essentially one that fails to grasp the nature of language, not one that has any *necessary* relationship to the characteristics of speech rather than writing. A proper grasp of speech situations, it could then be argued, would also not allow that error to arise, but theorists who focus on speech situations are more likely to make this error than theorists who focus on writing. This form of the argument would preserve the assertion that writing gives a clearer view of how language works than does speech but make unnecessary Derrida's claim that writing is prior to speech either temporally or logically and his subsequent struggle to avoid the insuperable problems of this claim by juggling terms and redefining speech as writing.

[16] Culler, *On Deconstruction*, p. 101. This does not, however, prevent Culler from acquiescing in all of Derrida's more specific claims; e.g., ". . . a concept of writing: a generalized writing that would have as subspecies a vocal writing and a graphic writing." It remains an odd fact that Culler saw the need to reformulate Derrida's point in a way that avoided devastating objections and yet did not explicitly object to those forms of the point that cannot survive those objections; is it by now too difficult for a deconstructionist publicly to reject an aspect of Derrida's thought, even when that aspect is unnecessary to and, in fact, separable from his major thrust?

To be sure, the beginning phase of Derrida's argument cannot be forgotten in any general appraisal of his ideas and his contribution to an understanding of language and meaning; but we can go on to examine the next development in his thought without being concerned that the failure of this first phase necessarily undermines what is to come. For in spite of the prominence that he and his expositors give this phase, and their strangely out-of-place moral crusade on behalf of writing, it neither lends support to nor detracts from the argument that follows. What his argument is really concerned with is a much more familiar issue, the relation of words to things, signs to referents, or, in its most traditional formulation, language to reality. Logocentrism, as Derrida calls the error he wishes to diagnose and transcend, is not about the priority of speech over writing but about the relationship of words to their referents.

One would expect Derrida's discussion now to have two aspects: (1) the diagnosis of logocentrism, its nature and its characteristic error, and (2) the exposition of a viewpoint that transcends the limitations of logocentrism. But before moving on to identify these two, it is necessary to point to a peculiarity of Derrida's position. In the case of most thinkers, we might think that (2) will represent more adequate ideas on language and (1) the necessary critique of others that precede them. First, one shows the need for better ideas; then, one moves on to expound those ideas. But this general scheme would not be an adequate account in Derrida's case: in his own accounts and equally in those of his followers, (1) always figures as a very central part of his view of language, and (2) is scarcely separable from it. This is an important matter: it means that the main *weight* of Derrida's ideas lies very much in their being an *antidote*, specifically an antidote to logocentrism, and a strong built-in presumption in the argument is that to recognize the shortcomings of logocentrism is *ipso facto* to see the need for his antidote, which emerges naturally from a recognition of those shortcomings. The positive aspect of the theory emerges from opposition to logocentrism: seeing its weakness is, apparently, the same thing as seeing that positive aspect.

Once again we see the same need for a dramatic and even moralistic stance that was visible in the discussion of speech and writing; logocentrism is not simply examined and discarded when found wanting, but denounced, and the sense of having triumphed over logocentrism must be retained as a strong positive element in the newer position to be taken. But this is a source of three major weaknesses we shall see in Derrida's argument. First, since the focus of his argument is on showing the shortcomings of logocentrism rather than on the process of developing an alternative, Derrida is effectively prevented from focusing on the choice between many possible alternatives to logocentrism: in his argument, transcending logocentrism and embracing his own viewpoint always seem to be one and the same thing—but they are not. Second, because he focuses so heavily on the need to overcome logocentrism, it is almost inevitable that he cannot acknowledge or deal with the fact that many other thinkers had already rejected it and gone on from there; thus existing alternatives are virtually ignored. And third, because in his argument transcending logocentrism is a step for which there is only one kind of rationale (his own), his critique of logocentrism is heavily infected with his as yet unargued position and its presuppositions, which therefore do not receive the full exposition they need. If the focus had been instead on situating, explaining, and justifying his argument as one of the many competing alternatives to logocentrism that now exist, these problems would have been avoided.

In view of all this, it is clearly necessary to consider Derrida's critique of logocentrism, not simply as the expression of his dissatisfaction with that theory, but as an integral part of his exposition of his own viewpoint. What, then, is logocentrism? The first thing that is always likely to be said is that this error consists in subscribing to a belief in the "metaphysics of presence." But how all of this is to be explained must be left to the words of Derrida and of those expositors who are generally accepted by deconstructionists as having given a good account of his thought. I have chosen a sample of the direct explanations that occur in both contexts:

[L]ogocentrism involves the belief that sounds are simply a representation of meanings which are present in the consciousness of the speaker.[17]

[A] metaphysical system that spans from Plato and Aristotle to Heidegger and Lévi-Strauss. . . . By Derrida this system is called "logocentric.". . . . As portrayed by Derrida, the logocentric system always assigns the origin of truth to the logos—to the spoken word, to the voice of reason or to the Word of God.[18]

[T]o focus attention on what I shall call *logocentrism:* the metaphysics of phonetic writing (for example, of the alphabet) which was fundamentally—for enigmatic yet essential reasons that are inaccessible to a simple historical relativism—nothing but the most original and powerful ethnocentrism, in the process of imposing itself upon the world, controlling in one and the same *order:* 1. The *concept of writing* in a world where the phoneticization of writing must dissimulate its own history as it is produced; 2. *the history of* (the only) *metaphysics,* which has . . . always assigned the origin of truth in general to the logos: the history of truth, of the truth of truth, has always been—except for a metaphysical diversion that we shall have to explain—the debasement of writing, and its repression outside "full" speech.[19]

[T]he "phonocentrism" that treats writing as a representation of speech and puts speech in a direct and natural relationship with meaning is inextricably associated with the "logocentrism" of metaphysics, the orientation of philosophy toward an order of meaning—thought, truth, reason, logic, the Word—conceived as existing in itself, as foundation.[20]

[17] Jonathan Culler, *Ferdinand de Saussure* (Harmondsworth, 1977), p. 119.
[18] Vincent Leitch, *Deconstructive Criticism* (New York, 1983), pp. 24–25.
[19] Derrida, *Of Grammatology,* p. 3.
[20] Culler, *On Deconstruction,* p. 92.

Here, then, are four accounts of what logocentrism is, all taken from writings either of Derrida or of individuals generally thought to convey an accurate sense of what he is saying. Note, also, that these are all *initial* explanations of the term in their context, that is, they are in each case the author's immediate explanation to the reader of what is meant by the strange new term.

Now, one thing is immediately conspicuous: considering the fact that a reader is in each case being introduced to a strange new term, the explanations offered are not very communicative, and they are also far from consistent in their emphases—an odd fact, when one thinks about other comparable situations in which new coinages in major theories are introduced. Usually, a major new coinage that is to represent a central term in a new way of thinking is given considerable attention: its meaning, its importance, and the need for the origination of a new term are the subject of a good deal of exposition. Yet this happens neither in Derrida's writings nor in those of his recognized expositors. Indeed, the examples I have chosen, judged against others, are if anything unusually explicit. Take, for example, the recent exposition of deconstruction by Christopher Norris. Norris is widely thought to be among the most faithful of all English-language expositors of deconstruction; a leading figure in the movement, Harold Bloom, hails his as "the most accurate" account of deconstruction available, while other reviewers have praised "Norris' remarkable success at presenting a clear and critical picture of central issues," attributed to him "much skill [in] the exposition of Derrida's teachings," and recommended his book as a particularly useful exposition.[21] But when the word *logocentrism* first appears in Norris's text, it is in a passage he cites from Derrida, without explanation of any kind. Here is the passage, now our fifth such:

The system of language associated with phonetic-alphabetic writing is that within which logocentric metaphysics, deter-

---

[21] These statements are made by Richard Kuczowski, *Library Journal* 17 (1982), p. 2098; by Harold Bloom on the dust jacket of Norris's book; and by John Sturrock in *Times Literary Supplement* (9 July 1982), p. 734.

mining the sense of being as presence, has been produced. This logocentrism, this *epoch* of the full speech, has always placed in parenthesis, *suspended*, and suppressed for essential reasons, all free reflection on the origin and status of writing.[22]

It takes another forty pages for Norris to mention the term in his own text, but even then with only the briefest possible explanation, which still leaves much unexplained: ". . . the logocentric myth is the craving for origins, truth and presence—which Derrida is everywhere at pains to uncover."[23] Norris, then, is far less explicit than any of the four examples I set out above; and though his exposition is designed as an *introduction* to deconstruction, it is clear that the key term *logocentrism* could not possibly be understood by anyone who needed an introduction to deconstruction. But it is not my purpose here simply to quarrel with Norris's account; I have introduced this example only to make a point that is essential to the further course of my argument. That point is the following: on looking at the four passages I have chosen to give a sense of the meaning of logocentrism, the reader might well feel that there must be clearer and better examples that I could have chosen. But there are none. There is, in fact, a bewildering lack of passages in deconstructive writings that explain the term through explicit comment on what it is and what it is not or with explanation of its distinctive character in and among the related ideas that occur in other writings on language and meaning.[24] The example of Norris, certainly a respected exposition, shows only that the alternatives I might have chosen were all worse—less communicative still—not better.

At this juncture, there is a strong tendency for Derrida's advocates to object that a demand for clarity begs the question at issue and violates the spirit of the deconstructive enterprise. I have already commented in the preceding chapter on the in-

---

[22] Derrida, *Of Grammatology*, p. 43; Norris, *Deconstruction*, p. 29.

[23] Norris, *Deconstruction*, p. 70.

[24] It would be tedious to demonstrate this point at length again for each of the technical terms of the deconstructive vocabulary, and I will therefore only say that the same holds for all of them: "supplement," "trace," etc.

consistency that is always present in this objection. But, interestingly enough, Derrida himself seems not to have any sympathy with it. On the matter of logocentrism and
phonocentrism he was, in his interview with Henri Ronse in
Positions, unequivocal: "I believe that I have explained myself
clearly on this subject."[25] But, in any case, it can scarcely be
maintained with any plausibility that an argument should proceed without a reasonably careful explanation of radically
new terms as soon as those new terms are introduced: how
else could that argument be understood? What, then, can we
make of logocentrism as explained in these four passages? The
first (by Culler) is so vague as to be nearly without content.
Depending on what we understand by "meanings present in
the consciousness of the speaker," it could be consistent with
almost any theory of meaning; whatever one's view of meaning, there will be some allowance in it for the fact that a
speaker is conscious of meaning something as he uses words.
Culler probably means that sounds are, for logocentric theorists, simply labels for concepts that are assumed to be formed
in the mind independent of language and thus are not dependent on a particular language for their content or structure; but
if so, his formulation does not explain this, and so the burden
of exposition is reversed: instead of having Culler explain the
idea to him, the reader must already know it to follow what
Culler is trying to explain.

The second, by Leitch, is unfathomable, for it treats as
equivalent four different entities and leaves it to the reader to
find the common element between them that must be the point
of the argument. But it is not clear what the voice of reason
and the spoken voice have in common—there are plenty of
irrational spoken voices. Nor is it clearer how and why the
voice of reason and the voice of God are bracketed; they are
often thought to be fundamentally opposed, as faith versus
secular rationalism.

Derrida's own explanation, the third, is obsessed with his
fruitless argument over the priority of writing and speech, an
argument that, as we have seen, he later abandons in effect

[25] *Positions*, p. 13.

when he has to redefine speech as writing in trying to rescue it. And aside from this, his only contribution to the understanding of logocentrism is the remark that it consigns the origin of truth to the logos. But that could mean anything, too, depending on what "origin" means and what "logos" means. There is a long history of theorizing about the relation of language and truth, and within that context Derrida's formulation is not specific enough to imply any particular position.

Only Culler's second version (my fourth above) gives us a fairly comprehensible, though still in many ways vague, account; logocentrism is not a fixation on words, as one might expect, but instead a belief that there is an order of meaning existing *independently* of the structure of any given language that is a foundation for all else. On the surface, the word *logocentrism* would not be a good name for the belief in question: for logocentrism here turns out to be much the same as the more familiar *essentialism*, the belief that words simply label real categories of meaning existing independently of a language. But in practice, a belief in immutable categories of meaning always involves a fixation on the words of the particular language spoken by the believer, which he mistakes for the categories of the "real" world. There are still real problems in the coherence even of this account of logocentrism by Culler. For example, when he speaks of the relation between speech and meaning in logocentric theory as "natural and direct," we can only wonder what a "natural and direct" relationship between speech and meaning could be, for it is obvious enough that the actual phonic shape of speech is arbitrary and conventional. Once more, the matter of speech versus writing misshapes the exposition.

The issue raised by this mention of an illusion of naturalness and directness is, in fact, misplaced by the recurring urge to pin the blame on speech and phonic material. The illusion of naturalism and directness that causes the problem in logocentrism lies not in the relation of speech and meaning but in the relation between meaning and reality: words (whether written or spoken) can seem to have a natural and direct relation to the structure of the world.

The overwhelming weight of further argument and com-

mentary both by Derrida and his expositors and commenta-
tors confirms that this is indeed the content of the concept *logocentrism*. A few examples will easily establish this. Frank
Lentricchia explains the point as follows: "Derridean deconstruction, more specifically, uncovers those rules governing
the production of all Western philosophical discourse which
would attempt to establish the signifier as a transparency
yielding an unobstructed view of a privileged and autonomous
signified (truth, reality, being)."[26] Hawkes uses a similar metaphor in explaining that deconstruction's " 'science of signs'
has demonstrated that the sign-system of language does *not*
act simply as a transparent window on to an established 'reality.' "[27] Fredric Jameson, too, explains the metaphysics of
presence engendered by logocentrism in similar fashion: "The
very problem of a relationship between thoughts and words
betrays a metaphysics of 'presence,' and implies an illusion
that universal substances exist, in which we come face to face
once and for all with objects; that meanings exist, such that it
ought to be possible to 'decide' whether they are initially verbal or not; that there is such a thing as knowledge which one
can acquire in some tangible or permanent way."[28] In all of
these accounts, the equation of logocentrism and the "metaphysics of presence" is clear;[29] the logocentric error is the illusion that reality and its ultimate categories are directly present to the mind, passed on by language without being shaped
or altered by it in any way whatsoever. Having come this far,
we can now see what Norris means when he glosses logocentrism as "the craving for origins, truth and presence." This
formulation is, in fact, a kind of shorthand for initiates even
though it is commonly offered as an explanation in introduc-
tions for the uninitiated. The terms need to be connected to
make sense: logocentrism is the illusion that the meaning of a
word has its *origin* in the structure of reality itself and hence

[26] Lentricchia, p. 177.

[27] Hawkes, p. 146.

[28] Frederic Jameson: *The Prison House of Language: A Critical Account of
Structuralism and Russian Formalism* (Princeton, 1972), p. 173.

[29] The equation of these two concepts is explicit also in Culler's essay on
Derrida in *Structuralism and Since*, ed. J. Sturrock (Oxford, 1979), p. 161.

makes the *truth* about that structure seem directly *present* to the mind. The point is that if one allows the terms of a given language to become so predominant in one's thinking that one can neither conceive of any alternative to them nor of any analysis that might question their coherence and sufficiency, one will inevitably come to believe that the words of that language reflect the necessary structure of the world: its categories will seem to be the world's categories, its concepts the structure of reality.

But now that the nature of the logocentric error is fully apparent, two serious questions present themselves: first, why does deconstruction make such a fuss about the discovery of a problem with which we were all familiar long before Derrida? And second, why the extraordinarily poor exposition of it in writer after writer? To anyone familiar with the history of thought on meaning and language these two points will inevitably seem related: if the logocentric error were stated in any clearer way it would be far too obviously an unoriginal discovery.[30] For this kind of thinking—that inherent in the referential theory of language, which holds that language simply refers to things in the world and labels them, or in essentialist thinking, which takes the concepts expressed in a language to be real essences existing independently of language—this sort of thought has been under attack and the subject of intense discussion for a very long time, but increasingly throughout this century.

When Derrida diagnoses and attacks this standpoint in linguistic theory he is surely a latecomer; and, in general, the belief of deconstructionists that they are attacking a superstition that still beguiles everyone seems quite out of touch with the reality of the twentieth century debate in theory of language.

[30] On this question of deconstruction's return to a more primitive view of language in order to justify its stance, cf. Graff, in his review of Culler's *The Pursuit of Signs*, in *London Review of Books* (3–16 September 1981): "Deconstruction provides elaborate proof that concepts can't pretend to be the things they stand for. But if one never supposed that concepts made this pretense, one might feel that it is the deconstructors who are promoting the confusion, perpetuating superstitions in order to justify this campaign against them."

Derrida is, in fact, attacking a view of meaning that by now would have to be counted a very naive and uninformed one;[31] for example, it has been dismembered in various ways, with varying emphases, by analytic philosophers such as Wittgenstein and others who have worked in his tradition, by linguists such as J. R. Firth, by anthropological linguists working in the tradition of Edward Sapir and Benjamin Lee Whorf, and by countless others. When, in 1966, Derrida began to denounce this kind of thinking as a *universal* error, he was demonstrating an extraordinary isolation from what had been happening for many years; and the mood of gleeful iconoclasm, revolutionary fervor, and avant-garde daring of the uniquely enlightened displayed by the followers of the deconstructionist banner contrasted strangely with the underlying reality that none of this could by now be considered remarkable or even unusual.

Perhaps Derrida might answer here that it is not possible to go beyond logocentrism and that, therefore, by definition, no preceding thinker can possibly have done so, in line with his assertion that "we cannot utter a single destructive proposition which has not already slipped into the form, the logic,

[31] Even Paul de Man's tracing the issue back to Nietzsche displayed no real widening of horizons. To be sure, Nietzsche in a brief essay complained of the metaphorical nature of all language and therefore of its inability to convey truth. But to single out Nietzsche in this way is justified only by the implicit claim that Nietzsche was either the first to express such a view (he was not) or that he was the most influential expounder of such a view before Derrida (also not so) or that his was the most sophisticated, complex, and logically well developed and worked out position of this kind before Derrida (again, obviously not true—Nietzsche's remarks on the subject were brief and undeveloped). More generally, there is still implicit in de Man's claim the belief that Derrida's move is a new, bold, and exciting one, rather than one that is familiar; and so, one must ask, what is the point of an attempt to discover and celebrate a nineteenth-century forerunner of Derrida in his rejection of logocentrism if Derrida's status in that regard is not unusual within the context of the twentieth century? See Paul de Man, "Nietzsche's Theory of Rhetoric," *Symposium* 28 (1974), pp. 33–51; Friedrich Nietzsche, "Über Wahrheit und Lüge im aussermoralischen Sinne," *Nietzsche: Werke, Kritische Gesamtausgabe*, ed. Georgio Colli and Mazzino Montinari (Berlin and New York, 1973), pt. 3, vol. 2, pp. 369–84.

and the implicit postulations of precisely what it seeks to contest."[32] But this would not help to answer the point I am making. If all attempts to go beyond essentialism can only remain attempts, Derrida's would still be only one that followed many others, and he therefore still owed it to us to place his own in the context of those rather than to claim a unique status for it as such an attempt, as if they had not existed. And there is here once again the problem that the structure of this disclaimer, too, is familiar enough: it has been said many times before that we can only use language and its conceptual system in trying to transcend it. There can, in fact, never be any substitute for a consideration of specific existing arguments and theories that are relevant to, compete with, or overlap with a proposal that asks to be considered a new one.

Moreover, this fact of Derrida's lack of originality in his diagnosis of and attack on essentialist thinking in theory of language is of greater than usual importance because of the prominence of this critique in his own ideas on language, and it is for this reason that I have stressed the unusually close connection of the negative and positive sides of his thought. There are two ways in which this lack of originality becomes, as a consequence of this connection, a special liability: first, the entire rhetorical position of deconstruction depends on its exploding myths and standing them on their head. It is offered essentially as an intellectually *liberating* force, so that what it negates is of independent importance in a way that is unusual in a philosophical or linguistic standpoint. Even if we conceded that Derrida's *alternative* to essentialist thinking were valuable, it would still be impossible for Derrida and his followers to see themselves as other than, first and foremost, iconoclasts and liberators. Deconstruction, it is constantly stressed, is disturbing and subversive. Deconstruction *must* find a prevalent unthinking belief to explode; if it cannot, and if it can only be construed as offering one particular suggested

[32] "Structure, Sign, and Play in the Discourse of the Human Sciences," in *The Structuralist Controversy*, ed. Richard Macksey and Eugenio Donato (Baltimore and London, 1972), p. 250.

alternative to logocentrism to be considered along with others, the special character to which it aspires is rendered impossible.

The second liability is closely related to the first. Since Derrida must focus on a prevalent superstition, and then overcome it, in order to fulfill a kind of general emotional demand of his program, he is effectively prevented from considering existing alternatives to his own counter to simple logocentrism. Derrida's explicit mention, in his essay "Structure, Sign and Play in the Discourse of the Human Sciences," of a few thinkers who, in his view, make some approach to "destructive" thinking only serves to confirm this point, rather than giving cause to weaken or modify it. For Heidegger, Freud, Nietzsche, and Lévi-Strauss (his choices) are nowhere near being central figures in the debate on this particular issue, and it is not difficult to see that Heidegger, Freud, and Lévi-Strauss all had a most unskeptical attitude to the sanctity of their own terminological innovations and the concepts they embodied. To mention such figures in this context only makes the absence of the many really central figures who deal directly and in a major way with essentialist thinking all the more obvious.

At this point we can see one more bad consequence of Derrida's characteristic rhetorical absolutism; for, it will be remembered, the "ethnocentrism" of phonocentrism, and by extension logocentrism, is said to exist "everywhere and always." No allowance is made in this formulation for even a single example of an enlightened thinker who rejected the superstition; their existence is categorically excluded. For Derrida, diagnosing and *overcoming* the superstition are too much part of the same process to allow his focus to shift to where at this stage in history it really belongs—not on the overcoming of the superstition but on the choice between many competing alternative ways of replacing it. Over and over again, Derrida's vocabulary makes the diagnosis of the error almost synonymous with the positive step; e.g., we must "put it in question" or see that it is "problematical." The real emotional force stays at that stage. This emerges with great clarity when Derrida says that "grammatology must deconstruct everything that ties the concept and norms of scientificity to onto-theology, logocentrism, phonologism. This is an immense and interminable work."[33] Again, Derrida's language claims a dramatic, even heroic, status for deconstruction—but more importantly, from the standpoint of its logic, he once more makes the dismantling of worn-out theories its focal point, so much so that this will be its interminable work; the next step will, in this formulation, never be reached.

But the real trouble here is that it is not enough to problematize, question, or stand logocentrism on its head. What we need is forward movement—and that means thought about the many possible *positive* steps and the choice between them. To pronounce something "problematical" is not a conclusion nor is it an intellectual achievement; when we do so, all we have done is point the way to a need for much more thought and analysis of the issues involved. It is not the end of a train of thought but a beginning. One does not rest at this point with a feeling of satisfaction that one has achieved the required intellectual breakthrough that allows things to seem more complex than they previously seemed, as deconstruction tends to do, but instead prepares to tackle the difficult job of finding the breakthrough that will begin to penetrate the problems now seen. The *real* intellectual work should begin now; pronouncing something problematical, or putting it in question, and then stopping there is far too easy. Moving on from an inadequate view such as essentialism will involve consideration of an infinite number of potential replacements of varying character. This means that even if deconstruction's seeming isolation from and innocence of the many existing alternatives to logocentric thinking did not preclude its examining them and weighing their relative strength, the general shape of its approach to the question would. Derrida's approach does not allow for investigating alternatives to his own counter to logocentrism, for there seems in his thought to be room only for one that is inseparable from and indeed identical with the act of exploding the myth of logocentrism. Per-

[33] *Positions*, p. 35.

haps the greatest general weakness of the deconstructive pattern of thinking is visible here—the tendency to place greatest emphasis on "putting in question" a given view, instead of moving on to search for a more viable idea representing a new and higher level of thought. The recurring tendency to think of all criticisms of deconstructionist ideas on language as logocentric in origin has the same source; the resistance to any awareness of other critiques of logocentrism means that all criticism of the deconstructive critique must be regarded as a return to logocentrism. There is no room in this framework of thought for the possibility that such criticism might come from the other direction.

On occasion, to be sure, an expositor of Derrida has noticed that logocentrism has been attacked before. Newton Garver, for example, in his preface to the English translation of *La voix et le phénomène*,[34] sees that the logocentric error diagnosed by Derrida really amounts to the theory of meaning inherent in logical positivism, and he thinks that Derrida's critique of it is analogous to Wittgenstein's. The theory in question is far more widespread than this, and attacks on it have come from many other quarters, too, but no matter—at least Garver has noticed that neither the diagnosis nor the attack are original. But there Garver stops, content to have been able to point out a parallel between Derrida and Wittgenstein but not willing to think further about what it means. Thus he

[34] Derrida, *Speech and Phenomena*, trans. David Allison, with an introduction by Newton Garver (Evanston, 1973). E.g., Derrida's rejection of private understanding is for Garver "an interesting parallel to the famous 'private-language argument' in Wittgenstein's *Philosophical Investigations*"; Derrida's deconstruction is "parallel with Wittgenstein's rejection of the idea of simples"; and Wittgenstein's idea that an expression has meaning only in "the stream of life," is also found by Garver in Derrida: "Derrida's central argument is an echo of Wittgenstein's extended and fascinating discussion" (pp. xvii; xxii; xxiii). Garver justly describes Wittgenstein's argument as famous but never faces the obvious issue that judgment must raise when Derrida shows no familiarity with it. A further problem in Garver's account is a degree of assimilation of Derrida to Wittgenstein's position that distorts Derrida; for while Derrida's starting point is similar to Wittgenstein's, his conclusions, as will be seen, are definitely not.

ignores the disturbing questions that the parallel should have caused him to ask: What now becomes of deconstruction's claim to be a revolutionary theory, a claim that is absolutely essential to its rhetorical and emotional stance, in fact to its very existence as an intellectually liberating phenomenon? Why does Derrida not acknowledge Wittgenstein's prior work or that of many others?[35] Why does Derrida introduce his

[35] Two further attempts to make the connection between Wittgenstein and Derrida have recently appeared, both seriously flawed, though for different reasons. While Newton Garver was concerned to make Derrida sound like Wittgenstein, Henry Staten's recent *Wittgenstein and Derrida* (Lincoln, Nebr., and London, 1984) goes at the matter the other way round: he attempts to make Wittgenstein sound like Derrida. The results are unconvincing, as Michael Fischer's review in *Philosophy and Literature* 10 (1986), pp. 93–97, justifiably insists. In general, Staten's procedure is to discuss a sequence of thoughts in Wittgenstein and translate them into Derridean terms, but in this process it is often apparent that he is failing to grasp what Wittgenstein's argument is about. His pages 69–74, for example, discuss Wittgenstein's commentary on the act of pointing at objects. What Wittgenstein is doing here is clear enough. One way of undermining the picture theory of language, according to which words are simply attached as labels to objects, is to consider ostensive definitions: this word refers to "that" (pointing) thing. Wittgenstein shows that ostensive definitions can never be simply ostensive, because it will not be clear to the person shown the meaning of a word by this process of pointing to its object just what is being pointed to: it could be a color, a surface, a shape, a place, a *type* or kind of object (antique, useful, wooden—or dozens more). All kinds of linguistic conventions, other contextual hints, and—the real point—linguistic interpretations come into play. All of this is designed to further the argument that words do not simply refer to things. Staten's comments show that he has not even begun to understand Wittgenstein's argument: "Wittgenstein wants a very literal description. . . . We can see here . . . an inability to pursue an abstract thought consistently because the thought keeps getting distracted by incidental features of physical surfaces." A tack different from both Garver (assimilating Derrida to Wittgenstein) and Staten (assimilating Wittgenstein to Derrida) is taken by Norris, in his recent *The Deconstructive Turn: Essays in the Rhetoric of Philosophy* (London and New York, 1983), pp. 34–58. Norris sees the gulf between Derrida's and Wittgenstein's overt doctrines that Garver and Staten both want to obliterate. But he maintains that "reading Wittgenstein with an eye to . . . figural language" will reveal ambivalences about his major intended themes that lead in the direction of deconstructive insights. Again, however, the examples given are always unconvincing. For example, at one point in his argument, Wittgenstein demonstrates with a negative example another aspect

viewpoint as *the* critique, exposure of, and antidote to logo-centrism instead of as an addition to and competition with other already existing critiques and alternatives to logocentrism? These appear to me unanswerable questions, and they cast a considerable shadow on the value of Derrida's contribution to the discussion of these matters.

So far, I have argued that the initial stage of Derrida's argument, which attempts to establish the priority of writing and speech, is both mistaken and unnecessary to his purposes; that his exposition of the logocentric viewpoint is neither coherent nor original; and that his rhetorical stance in discussing logocentrism necessarily involves a failure to acknowledge and deal with the current state of the debate on the issues he

---

of his general point about words having meaning not by being attached to things but by being part of a set of conventions. He considers the case of an arbitrary meaningless squiggle and says that it is possible to endow this, too, with meaning by imagining it as "a strictly correct letter of some foreign alphabet." The point is simple enough: we decide that a mark is meaningless *neither* by determining that it has no reference *nor* by looking at its own internal structure but rather when we abandon any possibility of its belonging to an organized sequence of other signs in a language convention. Norris seizes on this as "out of keeping with his general views" since the random cipher is taken up into an equally random language game of private associative meanings" (p. 52). But Wittgenstein's point is precisely the reverse—that to contemplate the cipher's having meaning would be to imagine it as an element in a foreign, i.e., public, language. Norris has falsely equated "imagined language" with "private language." Elsewhere, Norris takes Wittgenstein's point that incorrect spelling causes a feeling of uneasiness *not* to indicate the power of convention and habit in language, as one might expect, but instead to lead to the conclusion that graphic signs are "always and everywhere" (once more!) arbitrary, not only when they break with accepted convention (p. 51). "And this suggests in turn that language may be subjected to a generalized arbitrariness. . . ." Norris's conclusion as to Wittgenstein's drift here is certainly erroneous and is only achieved by confusing three different senses of arbitrary: (*a*) arbitrary = completely random, governed by no convention whatever (the case of incorrect spelling); (*b*) arbitrary = purely conventional (the case of correct spelling); and (*c*) arbitrary = with no fixed meaning (one deconstructive view of meaning). It hardly needs to be said that unease at incorrect spelling represents a reaction *against* the kind of arbitrariness that Norris wishes to see in Wittgenstein's text. Examples like these show well enough how forced Norris's reading of Wittgenstein has to be for him to see Derrida emerging from Wittgenstein's writings.

is raising. It remains to consider the one potentially positive element in Derrida's theory—his ideas advanced in response to logocentrism and their value among others that had already been suggested. What, then, does Derrida's particular counter to essentialist thinking and referential theories of meaning consist in, and what are its advantages, if any, when compared to others? For it is on *this* comparison that the value of Derrida's contribution depends, *not* on the comparison with that easy and outdated mark, logocentrism.

Derrida's view arises in the context of a critique of Saussure and is therefore only to be understood after a brief exposition of Saussure. Now Saussure himself was decidely anti-essentialist in his thinking, and Derrida largely admits as much; but he attempts to diagnose a flaw in Saussure's thinking through which, according to Derrida, he fell back into logocentrism after all.

Saussure rejected the notion that words simply reflected ideas and the inherent shape of the world with an argument that began by diagnosing two ways in which linguistic signs were arbitrary. First, the particular phonetic shape of a word was arbitrary: the concept *dog* in English could have been signaled by another combination of phonetic sounds without changing its meaning. This particular connection between sound and idea could have been otherwise, but if we are speaking English we must accept that language's arbitrary choice if we are to communicate in it. So far, Saussure is simply drawing attention to a commonplace. It is the second sense of "arbitrary" that is really interesting, however, for Saussure went on to say that *the concept itself* is an arbitrary creation of a language and does not necessarily exist outside that language. We might, for example, imagine a language in which there are the concepts *canine* (including foxes and wolves) but below that only *hounds*, *retrievers*, and so on. Is such a language simply defective, i.e., unable to reflect a fact of reality? The trouble is that the facts of reality are infinitely variable, and language must organize and simplify them if it is not to have one word for each new situation—an impossible notion in itself. Different languages group, organize, and even interpret them in different ways, and there is no possibility of avoiding arbitrariness in this process. But since concepts are nothing but the result of the process, concepts have an element of arbitrariness, too. Reducing an infinite world to a finite vocabulary can only be arbitrary in that sense.

Saussure says that because of this arbitrariness in the conceptual system of a language, its concepts are not simple, positive terms that achieve their meaning by corresponding to reality or to nonlinguistic facts; instead, they achieve their meaning by the place they take within the system of concepts of the language and, in particular, by their function in differentiating one category of things from another. It is the system of differentiation, therefore, that is the source of meaning: the way in which a language simplifies an infinitely complex set of phenomena to make up a finite set of categories, to one or other of which all phenomena will be assigned. What then becomes important is the particular set of characteristics that are the basis of the differentiation introduced by the set of concepts.

Take, for example, the series of words used in English for the temperature of water. The full spectrum of temperature goes from 0 degrees to 100 degrees Celsius, but the number of different temperature readings is infinite; our choice of one hundred points on the scale is already a simplification for our convenience, and an arbitrary one, in that we could choose ten or twenty or any other number. But when we then use the words *cold*, *warm*, *hot*, and *scalding*, we are simplifying even further. *Warm water* is, then, in one sense not a fact of nature; it represents instead a decision of the English language to cut up the spectrum in a particular, arbitrary way. There is no concept *warmness* outside of the language, and the meaning of that word derives not primarily from its reflecting reality but rather from its place in the system of terms, its differentiating *warm* from *hot*. Interestingly, the arbitrariness (in Saussure's defined sense) is further highlighted if we look at the closely related cognates in German. For while the words may look the same, they are not; the transition from the German word *warm* to *heiss* occurs very much further up the scale than is the case in the transition from *warm* to *hot*. The transition marks the *upper* end of the comfort zone in German (*heisses Wasser* is almost *too* hot) while it marks the lower end in English (hot water is hot *enough*). An English speaker who learns the similar German words without realizing that the two *systems* are different is likely to get hurt. A German speaker, on the other hand, going at the matter from the other direction, is likely to end up with a bath he will think rather too cold. What, then, is the concept *warmness* of water? It is a creation of the English language, a decision on its speakers' part to group together and regard as equivalent for a certain purpose everything from roughly 90 degrees to 115 degrees Fahrenheit. Water itself does not dictate such a choice, but only the arbitrary system of a given language; and it is the transition points, to *cold* and to *hot*, and thus the differences between the three terms, that determine meaning.

It is easy to draw completely false conclusions from Saussure's argument.[36] For example: the fact that *warmness* as a

[36] The most common and widely quoted misconception is that contained in the short, very confused account of Saussure in Emile Benveniste's essay "Nature du signe linguistique," part of his *Problèmes de Linguistique Générale* (Paris, 1966). Benveniste thinks that Saussure's concept of the sign omits the crucial matter of language's reference to the real world and sees proof of this in Saussure's (alleged) covert reliance on this reference to reality whenever he talks of concepts, in spite of his insistence that they are psychological, not real, entities: "En réalité Saussure pense toujours, quoiqu'il parle d''idée,' à la représentation de *l'objet réel* et au charactère évidemment non néccessaire, immotivé, du lien qui unit le signe à la *chose* signifiée" ("In reality, although Saussure always talks about an 'idea,' he is always thinking of the representation of the *actual object* and of the obviously contingent, unmotivated connection between the sign and the *thing* signified"; *Problèmes de Linguistique Générale*, p. 54). According to Benveniste, then, when Saussure tells us that the arbitrariness of the signifier is shown by the fact that French has "boeuf" where German has "Ochs," (both being attached to the same signified), he betrays the fact that he is just thinking of the same reality, the same actual animal, that exists on both sides of the international border. But here Benveniste's own naive realism has not allowed him to grasp what Saussure is saying, for there is nothing inconsistent here: Saussure's point is not just that similar animals exist in France and Germany but that a similar *conception* of them exists in both places. Another example from Benveniste that shows how his diagnosis of an illegitimate intrusion of "reality" in Saussure results from

concept is a creation of the English language does *not* mean
that warmness has nothing to do with reality or that statements that include reference to warmness are only statements
about the English language, not about the world. On the contrary, variations in temperature must exist and be perceptible

a misreading of Saussure's text occurs when he tells us that Saussure declares
"que la nature du signe est arbitraire parce qu'il n'a avec le signifié 'aucune
attache naturelle dans la realité' " ("that the nature of the sign is arbitrary
because it has 'no natural connection in reality' with the signified"; p. 50).
But Saussure's text says something quite different: "Le signifiant . . . est *immotivé*, c'est-à-dire arbitraire par rapport au signifié, avec lequel il n'a aucune
attache naturelle dans la realité" ("The signifier . . . is *unmotivated*, i.e., arbitrary in its relation to the signified, with which it has in reality no natural
connection"; *Cours de Linguistique Générale*, Paris, 1981, p. 101). Benveniste has confused "signe" and "signifiant" and as a result takes Saussure to
be talking about the relation of signs to reality; but the "realité" of Saussure's
sentence has nothing to do with the reality of things but only with the lack of
any natural connection between sound and concept. Saussure is talking only
of the fact that there is no real reason why a particular word/idea should have
this sound rather than that. Nonetheless, Benveniste's position is the basis of
much commentary on Saussure; for example, Robert Scholes's recent account, though not mentioning Benveniste, adopts essentially the same position, if anything even more incautiously: "The Saussurean formulation, like
many 'linguistic' views of language, eliminates the third term [reference, or
objects] and with this gesture erases the world" (*Textual Power*, New Haven,
1985, p. 92). And this very serious misconception about Saussure finally leads
him to *equate* Saussure and Derrida: "(1) Are all signs linguistic signs? (2) Are
linguistic signs purely linguistic—that is, are verbal meanings sustained entirely by relations among words, or are relations with nonverbal entities also
involved? Saussure, Derrida, and his followers like to go as far as possible in
the direction of answering both of those questions affirmatively" (p. 102).
Scholes's suggestion that in Saussure's thought relations with nonverbal entities are not involved in the meanings of words represents, it must be insisted,
a complete and comprehensive misunderstanding of Saussure. Saussure's replacing the traditional pairing of words and things with the triad of sounds,
concepts, and reality represents a redefining of the way words relate to the
world, not an abolition of that relationship. This curious refusal to deal with
what Saussure really said appears to me to occur because, when Saussure attempts to redefine the relationship between language and reality, he apparently triggers a reflex reaction of fear that that relationship is being cut completely, and outraged naive realism strikes back without thinking about what
has really been said. Only so visceral, and therefore unthinking, a reaction
could make Saussure and Derrida seem identical on this point.

to allow the contrast between *warm* and *hot* to *mean anything*. If the words only told us something about English without also telling us what the actual conditions were that made the use of one rather than the other an appropriate and correct use of English, then they could not tell us anything about English either: English would not exist. It works both ways: the word *warm* gives us information about our language only given our recognizing temperature variations. And the word *warm* gives us information about the world only given our ability to understand and use English. *It is just as wrong to say that warmth is simply a fact of nature as it is to say that warmth is simply a fact about language*; and the greatest error of all would be to assume that the falsity of the first of these alternatives required us to turn to the second. But as we shall see, this is a typical deconstructive error—one engendered by the persistent habit of denouncing a superstition and looking to its polar opposite in order to complete the denunciation. Unfortunately, these two positions are not opposites, in the sense that one must be right if the other is wrong, but instead equivalents, being two different versions of the *same* logical error.

An equally false conclusion, only possible if Saussure's point is completely misunderstood, is that the arbitrariness of the sign makes meaning arbitrary in the sense of indeterminate. To the contrary: it is precisely the fact that the conceptual system of English is the common property of its speakers (i.e., that all in a sense agree to make the same arbitrary decision) that gives its words any meaning at all. As Saussure himself puts it, "The word *arbitrary* . . . should not imply that the choice of the signifier is left entirely to the speaker (we shall see below that the individual does not have the power to change a sign in any way once it has been established in the linguistic community)," and "The arbitrary nature of the sign explains in turn why the social fact alone can create a linguistic system. The community is necessary if values that owe their existence solely to usage and general acceptance are to be set up; by himself, the individual is incapable of fixing a single

49

value."[37] Arbitrariness in this sense, then, refers not to randomness but to the reverse, to the fact that there is a *definite agreement* on the particular system of terms to be used and on how they are to be used. It does not mean that the meaning of a given *word* is arbitrary, for unless that word has a place in a system of terms, there is no system, no agreement, no meaning, and thus no language and no communication.

This brief exposition has been designed to give a sense of what Saussure means when he says that in language there are no positive terms (i.e., terms with inherent meaning outside the system) but only differences—like the difference between *warm* and *hot*—with meaning established by those differences.

Derrida uses Saussurean terminology to develop his own ideas, preserving especially Saussure's key terms *difference*, *signifier*, and *signified*. Since it is important to make sure that what we are discussing is really Derrida and not a summary that may have changed his emphases in small but significant ways, I shall set out a number of key passages from his writings:

> The play of differences supposes, in effect, syntheses and referrals that forbid at any moment, or in any sense, that a simple element be *present* in and of itself, referring only to itself. Whether in the order of spoken or written discourse, no element can function as a sign without referring to another element which itself is not simply present. This interweaving results in each "element"—phoneme or grapheme—being constituted on the basis of the trace within it of the other elements of the chain or system. This interweaving, this textile, is the *text* produced only in the transformation of another text. Nothing, neither within the elements nor within the system, is anywhere ever simply present or absent. There are only, everywhere, differences and traces of traces.[38]

[37] Ferdinand de Saussure, *Course in General Linguistics*, pp. 68–69 and 113.

[38] *Positions*, p. 26.

[I]n the absence of a center or origin, everything became discourse . . . that is to say, a system in which the central signified, the original or transcendental signified, is never absolutely present outside a system of differences. The absence of the transcendental signified extends the domain and the play of signification infinitely.[39]

One could call *play* the absence of the transcendental signified as limitlessness of play, that is to say as the destruction of onto-theology and the metaphysics of presence.[40]

[T]he meaning of meaning (in the general sense of meaning and not in the sense of signalization) is infinite implication, the indefinite referral of signifier to signified.[41]

This field is in effect that of *play*, that is to say, a field of infinite substitutions. . . . One could say . . . that this movement of play, permitted by the lack or absence of a center or origin, is the movement of *supplementarity*.[42]

The maintenance of the rigorous distinction—an essential and juridical distinction—between the *signans* and the *signatum*, the equation of the *signatum* and the concept, inherently leaves open the possibility of thinking a *concept signified in and of itself*, a concept simply present for thought, independent of a relationship to language, that is of a relationship to a system of signifiers. By leaving open this possibility—and it is inherent even in the opposition signifier/signified, that is in the sign—Saussure contradicts the critical acquisitions of which we were just speaking. He accedes to the classical exigency of what I have proposed to call a "transcendental signified," which in and of itself, in its essence, would refer to no signifier, would exceed the chain of signs, and would no longer itself function as a signifier. On the contrary, though, from the moment that one questions the possibility of such a transcendental signified, and that

---

[39] *Writing and Difference*, trans. Alan Bass (Chicago, 1978), p. 280.
[40] *Of Grammatology*, p. 50.
[41] *Writing and Difference*, p. 25.
[42] Ibid., p. 289.

one recognizes that every signified is also in the position of a signifier, the distinction between signified and signifier becomes problematical at its root.[43]

Using this basic framework of Saussure's theory and its terminology, then, Derrida develops his own ideas. Saussure had argued that meaning is not a matter of sounds being linked to concepts existing outside a given language but instead arises from specific contrasts between terms that are differentiated in specific ways. Derrida's first move is to introduce the word *play* and substitute it for a word such as *contrast*, so that now we have the play of differences as the source of meaning. *Play* is no longer a matter of specific contrasts—it is (to use the vocabulary of the passages I have cited) "limitless," "infinite," and "indefinite"; and thus meaning has become limitless, infinite, and indefinite. This thrust is developed with both spatial and temporal ideas. Since play is ceaseless, it is temporally extended; by playing on the two meanings of the French verb *différer*—to differ and to defer—Derrida argues that the play of differences means that meaning is not present to us but is *deferred*, i.e., postponed into a future rather than a present.[44] And the spatial sense of "present" comes into his notion that the absence of an independent concept ("transcendental signified," as he calls it) means that meaning is never present to us. The words *supplement* and *trace* are now introduced to reinforce the idea that no single final act of perceiving meaning is possible—the extended and indefinite play of differences will introduce supplements and uncover "traces" of them. Meaning accumulates endlessly. There is one more step in the transformation of Saussure's terminology: in this infinite process, "signifieds" (i.e., concepts) can be in the position of "signifiers." And the infinite extension of the process of signification is identified with another fateful notion: everything

---

[43] *Positions*, pp. 19–20.

[44] Derrida elaborates this idea most fully in the essay "Différance," the closing chapter of his *La Voix et Le Phénomène* (translated under the title *Speech and Phenomena*).

becomes discourse, i.e., since we are cut off from ultimate referents, there is only language.

What, then, are we to make of Derrida's suggested counter to essentialist thinking? The most obvious thing about it is the many unjustified leaps in the argument. Many times there is assertion without argument or justification; a term is sometimes substituted for another, as if they were equivalent, when a difference between the two makes a considerable (but not argued or supported) difference to the argument, and Saussurean terminology is used with non-Saussurean meanings, again without explanation or rationale being given. The most obvious gaps in Derrida's argument are the following:

1. Saussure had said that meaning is created by the opposition of terms, that is, by *specific* differences. Derrida imports into this scheme the word *play*, which immediately says a great deal more, but that word is introduced into his text without any argument for what it suggests; it is introduced casually, as if only a more colorful term were involved. But *play* has already suggested that the mechanism of differentiation is much less controlled and specific than it was before the word was introduced. Having done this, Derrida then completes the movement of his argument with the introduction of "limitless," "indeterminate," and "infinite," now making the implications of *play* quite explicit and taking them to an extreme.[45] This is a very radical new turn in Saussure's argument—and yet Derrida allows his prose to introduce these new terms as if they were simply linguistic flourishes and the expression of an energetic, forceful style—there is no pause to explain why he or we should accept the substance of what is being said. And, indeed, the result is

[45] It is sometimes said that this point of Derrida's is supported by the fact that a dictionary explains words by using other words; but this is an entirely different matter. Dictionaries presuppose a *general* mastery of a language to explain specific items within it; and the proof of this is that anyone who picks up a dictionary of Hungarian without knowing any Hungarian will not be enlightened by it in any way.

not an extension or correction of Saussure's argument but a garbling of it. For if we use Saussure's notion of *differences* and try to extend it with the notion of a limitless, indefinite play of differences, we only succeed in reducing the notion to meaninglessness. If terms can play (a) indiscriminately against all other terms and (b) endlessly and indeterminately rather than specifically, the result would be nothing—no specific contrasts that generate meaning, no significant differences forming systems, nothing identifiable or recognizable to anyone, hence no communication and no meaning at all. To see a difference between things is to see specific qualities uniquely contrasted with each other. To see unspecific, indeterminate differences is a contradiction—it is to see nothing. Saussure's point was that languages are a repository of very specific decisions to divide up the endless continuum of experience into arbitrarily defined and demarcated, i.e., differentiated, units and to make a finite system out of what was infinite. When Derrida uses Saussure's terms to argue that signification is a matter of *infinite* play, he is doing something inconsistent with those terms. He has returned us from the finite system of a language to the infinite—to what was there before a language coalesced "arbitrary" decisions to reduce it to a finite system. He has abolished language, not redefined it. Difference and differentiating are inseparable from specific, finite, definite decisions. If anyone takes *black* as playing against every other word in English, indiscriminately, then he does not understand its meaning. It is when he knows that a uniquely relevant contrast is with *white* and also knows how that linguistic contrast is relevant to the corresponding contrasts in visual experience, that we are sure he understands it. The notion of infinite and indiscriminate play is impossible in any context that requires distinctiveness; signification and differentiation both constitute such a context.

2. The notion that the passage of *time* is an essential part of a word's achieving its meaning (i.e., deferral of

meaning, postponing of meaning, infinite extending of meaning) rests on a misunderstanding of the process of making choices among words, and it in any case only arises from Derrida's play on two quite separable meanings of the French verb *différer* rather than from any logical argument; the notion of a continuing process of the play of signs in the production of meaning is, in fact, a red herring, having nothing to do with the nature of meaning at all. As we shall see, Derrida has confused the process of meaning with the analysis of that process. The meaning of one word does indeed depend on the meaning of many others; but to choose one word from a system is to employ *all* of the systematic contrasts with other words at that very moment—the process of contrasting does not stretch out into the future. It would follow from Derrida's account that when I use a given word, I set in motion a process, in my mind and those of my listeners, of going through all of the other possibilities one by one until I have meant all that I could have meant by all of the contrasts involved. (The case is worse given the limitless, infinite play of terms that Derrida postulates, rather than the specific, limited contrasts with which language actually works.) But that is absurd: no one ever does this or needs to. When choosing one, I *have done* all the work involved in not choosing the other, and my act has all of the meaning it can have straight away. Other kinds of systematic choices illustrate the same point. When I move a rook in chess, part of the meaning of that move lies in a rook's *not* being a knight and so on. But it is unnecessary for me and my opponent mechanically to go through a process of thinking "it was not a knight, it was not a pawn, etc.," exhausting all possibilities, before grasping what I have done; all of that is already grasped in knowing what a rook move is. Derrida is evidently confusing signification and the analysis of signification. The full *analysis* of all of the ways in which a word functions in a language can indeed stretch out into the future. Similarly, the full *analysis* of the impact of a chess move can take forever, but that impact

55

itself is achieved immediately with the move. Defining a word might take weeks of careful thought, but the full use of it is achieved immediately upon that use. Analysis of an action may involve a span of time running into a potentially infinite future, then, but the action itself is still made in its entirety at a specific point in time; its consequences and ramifications may belong to the future, but its character is set once it is made. Derrida's attempt to introduce the elapsing of time to make the meaning of a word infinitely extensible is therefore unsuccessful.

3. Derrida's spatial argument from physical presence or absence is just as much of a red herring as his temporal argument for meaning extending into the future. All words are, in a sense, present for possible choice, and then all but one rendered absent by the actual choice; that is how language works. The absence is not something that necessitates a search or a diagnosis of absent meaning; absence *is* meaning when a systematic choice is made. Derrida's terms *trace* and *supplement* both rely heavily on his spatial and temporal metaphors (e.g., presence/absence, deferral); without these supports, the two terms have no place in linguistic theory.

4. The notion that "everything becomes discourse" is essentially the error that I have noted above—the leap from one common mistake of supposing that *warm* is simply a fact of nature to that of the opposite, but logically similar, mistake that *warm* is simply a fact of language.

These substantive objections to Derrida's revision and extension of Saussure's argument are surely decisive. But Derrida's method of advancing his argument by unsupported assertions and bold linguistic flourishes deserves comment here, too. There are reasons to object to the substitution of *play* for *opposition*, for example, and I have stated them. But it is also relevant to say, why should we simply accept Derrida's unsupported introduction of the word *play*, and what reason can *he* give us for doing so?

This argument by unsupported assertion is nowhere more

evident then when Derrida attempts to prove that Saussure was a closet logocentrist, in the last of the passages I have cited above. Here, Derrida tells us that Saussure's maintaining a distinction between signified and signifier, and equating signified with concept, leaves open the possibility of a transcendental signified, a concept independent of language. To this, it is only necessary to say, why? and how? Since Saussure has spent a great deal of time showing that a concept-in-itself is impossible, Derrida owes us an explanation of this point; but all we get is the strange assertion that, when we see that every signified is also in the position of signifier, the distinction between signifier and signified "becomes problematical." The distinction would indeed become "problematical" if it no longer existed—if, as Derrida asserts, signifieds can be signifiers! But just *how* does the distinction break down? And how does that lead us to a concept-in-itself? One is left with a sense that a startling assertion is tossed out and of the reader being dared to question it, for no support or explanation is given. The habit of leaving unanswered questions and unexplained assertions with the conclusion that something has "become problematical" is found frequently in Derrida and in deconstructive writings generally. But the problems in what has been asserted can not be avoided so easily; consider, for example, the following:

1. What can it possibly mean to say that a signified can also be a signifier? Saussure had introduced "signifier" as the phonic shape or distinctive sound of a word and "signified" as the idea content of that word. A sound is, obviously, not an idea, so that Saussure's distinction is clear and effective. A signifier can not be a signified in that sense. Is Derrida using Saussure's terms with a different definition of them? He does not say. If not, how can an idea become a sound—surely so odd an idea that it deserves some exposition. To be sure, Derrida often returns to this question and talks about it but without real explanation. Take, for example, his further comments in *Positions*: "[N]or is it a question of confusing at every

57

level, and in all simplicity, the signifier and the signified. That this opposition or difference cannot be radical or absolute does not prevent it from functioning, and even from being indispensable within certain limits—very wide limits."[46] But once more, these remarks remain very general: the distinction in question has been pronounced "indispensable," "not radical or absolute," and "problematical," but after all of this we still await the specific demonstration of what it means and how it is possible to say that a signified (concept) can be in the position of a signifier (sound-shape).

2. Why does Derrida equate "language" and "a system of signifiers"? If we are using Saussure's terms, this is a plain error—a language is a system of *signs*, with each sign consisting both of signifier (sound-shape) and signified (concept). Language is obviously more than phonetics and phonemics. Has Derrida misunderstood Saussure's terms, or is he redefining them? Some light may be shed on this point, however, by Derrida's remarks on Saussure's theory of language in *Positions*.[47] Twice Derrida cites Saussure's statement that "in its essence [the linguistic signifier] is not at all phonic," without citing the succeeding phrase in Saussure's text: "but incorporeal—constituted not by its material substance but by the differences that separate its sound-image from all others." Saussure is saying, of course, that the signifier is not phonetic but phonemic, i.e., still in the realm of sound but constituted by *distinctive* sound-patterns, not raw acoustic properties. But on both occasions, Derrida continues with comments that indicate that he has misunderstood what Saussure is saying and thus what "signifier" means for Saussure. In the first instance, Derrida draws the conclusion that the signifier for Saussure is "therefore . . . no longer in a privileged or exclusive way phonic"; in the second, Derrida goes on to assert that, although Saussure says that the signifier is not

[46] *Positions*, p. 20.
[47] Ibid., pp. 18 and 21.

at all phonic, he "had to privilege speech, everything that links the sign to phoné." Both these passages suggest that Derrida takes Saussure to be saying that the signifier is not constituted by sound at all, that is, it is neither phonetic nor phonemic. For example, the structure "although for Saussure the signifier is not phonic, he privileges speech" makes "phonic" and "speech" parallel. The substitution of "phonemic" for "not phonic" (a legitimate and necessary equation in Saussure's statement) would make nonsense of the structure of Derrida's statement; it would then read "although for Saussure the signifier is phonemic, he privileges speech." The word *although* obviously makes no sense here; and from this one may conclude that Derrida failed to understand that Saussure was excluding only the *phonic*, not the *phonemic*, from the nature of the signifier. The same point holds for the other context. Here Derrida obviously takes "phonic" to contrast with "writing" when he says that Saussure refuses to privilege the phonic. But that is not Saussure's contrast; he is contrasting, not phonic and graphic, but phonic and phonemic. What emerges from these remarks is that Derrida has fundamentally misunderstood Saussure's term "signifier." This raises the possibility that what is really happening here is that Saussure's system of three elements (signifier, signified, referent) is sometimes being confused with the more popular, but more primitive, two-element system of words and their referents. To call language a system of signifiers would make sense only within that more primitive system, that is, if signifiers were understood as words or as what Saussure calls signs. (In Saussurean terminology, language is a system of signs, with each sign having two aspects, a signifier and a signified.) Perhaps, then, this basic confusion about Saussure's system of thought is a source of the assertion that language is a system of signifiers.

3. Why does Derrida say that the hypothetical "transcendental signified" would no longer itself function as a signifier? A concept, divorced from language or not,

could not function as a sound. There is no explanation for this strange and (in the absence of explanation) seemingly nonsensical assertion.

4. Why does Saussure's distinction between signifiers and signifieds—seemingly unavoidable given his use of the terms—imply a transcendental signified? Saussure has explained that a concept can only exist if it is part of a differentiated system of concepts, i.e., without differentation there is nothing distinguished, and therefore no concept defined, and no meaning. How is this argument insufficient?[48] We are not told, and Derrida's assertion about Saussure's inconsistency on this point therefore remains baffling.

For all of these reasons, then, Derrida's ideas on meaning and language do not achieve any real coherence or force. Before proceeding, however, I must deal with an attempt made by one of deconstruction's expositors to put the matter in a different light, one that might (or so it is hoped) seriously change the basis on which such judgments could be made. Jonathan Culler argues that Derrida does not commit himself to the ideas on meaning that we have seen in the passages I have cited from his writings.[49] Culler points out that Derrida speaks of two views of interpretation and says that "Derrida has often been read as urging us to choose the second interpretation, to affirm a free play of meaning. . . . The notion of the 'free play of meaning' has had a fine career, particularly in

---

[48] Culler's attempt to explain and justify Derrida's charge that Saussure is a covert logocentrist produces the vaguest and most inconsequential pages of his book *Ferdinand de Saussure*. Culler himself seems to know as much, for he concludes, "Attempts to challenge logocentrism involve a host of extremely complex problems. . . . My remarks here simply give some indications of the line of argument" (p. 123). Culler also draws out the implications of Derrida's pronouncing language a system of signifiers—but accepts them: "The reality of signs is no longer to be identified in the signified, which is intangible and irrecoverable, but in the signifier" (p. 120). And so, apparently, the reality of language is to be limited to sound-shapes, excluding concepts or ideas—a position that is surely difficult to take seriously.

[49] Culler, *On Deconstruction*, pp. 131–34.

America." (The first of the two interpretations is, of course, that which "dreams of deciphering a truth or an origin," i.e., the logocentric interpretation discussed above.) Culler is clearly correct in saying that Derrida has "often" been interpreted this way, and indeed he could have put the point more strongly—this interpretation is nearly universal. This might not be surprising, given the passages I have cited from Derrida. But Culler cites another, in which Derrida says that one cannot make a firm choice between the two interpretations: "I do not for my part believe, although these two interpretations must accentuate their difference and sharpen their irreducibility, that there can today be any question of *choosing*. . . ." Culler concludes that, for Derrida, meaning has a "double character." Should any of this change the evaluation we have made of Derrida's ideas on meaning? I think not, for the following reasons:

1. Whether it is one of two viewpoints we must entertain or simply one by itself, the free play of meaning is an incoherent idea, and the analysis and criticisms of it which I have made still stand. Choosing an incoherent idea by itself or accepting it as one of two incoherent ideas is equally unwise; and expounding and advancing for serious attention an incoherent idea is untenable whether it comes by itself or with another.

2. The same holds for logocentrism: it remains an incoherent idea, one long since discarded by philosophers of language, and would be so whether offered by itself or as a package together with its polar opposite.

3. Culler's observation, and the passage he cites from Derrida, are, to be sure, entirely consistent with the deconstructive logic of "neither/nor and either/or," which I have commented on above; and the same objections apply. If *both* positions are uninteresting and incoherent, nothing has been achieved by embracing both rather than one. The simple fact that there are two, and that they are polar opposites, by itself does nothing to make either one, or both together, worth anything.

4. Followers of Derrida can surely be forgiven for abstracting from his work a practical preference for the second in view of, on the one hand, the persistent denunciation of the first as limited and ethnocentric, the ground of common sense and unreflectiveness, and, on the other hand, the extensive discussion, always positive in tone, of the second.

What Culler misses here is that, while Derrida puts forward the idea of a duality as a general principle, when he gets down to developing the two interpretations themselves the overwhelming weight of his discussion favors the second; his followers were not really imagining the fundamental thrust they see in the working out of the idea of play in meaning. Derrida's emphases are, in fact, inconsistent; one passage is hard to square with another. Nor is the notion of *free* play their invention, as he implies; it occurs many times in the much quoted essay "Structure, Sign and Play in the Discourse of the Human Sciences."

In the preceding discussion, I have pointed both to outright mistakes in Derrida's argument and to gaps in the argument where explanation and support were obviously needed for assertions that, on their face, seemed implausible and full of logical problems. What is profoundly troubling, however, is that these assertions are repeated by followers and expositors generally without showing any awareness of the fact that they raise serious problems that require comment and explanation. Now, there may be nothing very unusual about a writer's occasionally missing out a step in his argument or failing to explain what is obvious to him but may not be so to anyone who is less close to his idea—though in Derrida's case, this is more than an occasional occurrence; but what is truly unusual is that his expositors seem never to notice these gaps. For example, in expositions of deconstruction, it is repeated over and over that a signified can also be a signifier and that language is a system of signifiers.[50] But none of the writers con-

---

[50] For example, Lentricchia cheerfully asserts that "by his [Derrida's] refusal to accept uncritically the Western metaphysics of the sign . . . Derrida

cerned seems to be aware that *much* explanation will be needed if one makes such statements and that the informed reader's immediate objections will need to be answered. This leads to the disturbing thought, are writers without such an awareness in a position to discuss these matters at all?

Not surprisingly, this has helped to allow a wholesale garbling of Saussurean terminology and a general degeneration of discussion in this area. Many examples can be cited, and they are by no means from obscure figures among deconstructionist scholars. Alan Bass, for example, the major translator of Derrida's work (four volumes have been translated by Bass to date), tells us that "the essence of Saussure's work in linguistics is his doctrine of the arbitrary or unmotivated relationship between signifier and signified."[51] This is simply and appallingly wrong. Well nigh all linguists, before Saussure and since, have understood that the relationship between the vocal sounds of "apple" and the idea to which it is connected is arbitrary, if for no other reason than that the French *pomme* is arbitrarily connected to a similar idea by a different group of speakers. Saussure's importance lay in something far more interesting and far more unique to him: he saw a *second* arbitrariness, the arbitrariness of the structure of the concept "apple" and its relation to the physical objects. Yet this error, and derivatives of it, permeate most deconstructive writings. Ter-

---

collapses all signifieds within signifiers" (p. 168), without further explanation, thus putting forward a baffling view without showing any awareness of the enormity of its problems or the pressing need to face them. This is, in any case, inaccurate; Derrida never says that he "collapses all signifieds into signifiers"; on the contrary, he puts the distinction in question and pronounces it problematical but also essential—for what that is worth. Even more remarkable is Lentricchia's overall judgment of Derrida's discussion and extension of Saussure: "Especially in the reading of Saussure, the scholarly force of Derrida's argument is irresistible." When measured against the reality of what actually happens in that reading, this judgment seems to me an astonishing one.

[51] Alan Bass, " 'Literature'/Literature," in *Velocities of Change*, ed. Richard Macksey (Baltimore and London, 1974), p. 343. Bass's translations have included *The Post Card* (1987), *Margins of Philosophy* (1982), *Positions* (1981), and *Writing and Difference* (1978).

ence Hawkes argues that Derrida's purpose is to undermine
the notion that "*necessary* connections exist between signifier
and signified."[52] The attribution now to Derrida of what Bass
attributed to Saussure (but which is really a commonplace
barely worth attributing to anyone) in itself indicates the
depths of conceptual confusion in this discussion. If Hawkes
and Bass take this to be a central new idea, whether in Saussure or Derrida, it must be because they have taken the signi-
fier/signified distinction in Saussure to be the same as that between words and things; but that would be a misconception
so fundamental as to be disabling: how can one contribute to
a discussion without any grasp of its most basic ideas? When
Leitch tells us, with heavy emphasis and as if expounding a
profound new idea, that words and things are *different*, the
source of his misconception is obviously the same;[53] but now
we see a use of a key Saussurean term—difference, differentiation—in almost comically inappropriate fashion. The point of
"difference" in Saussure lies, of course, in the differentiation
of words from other words and ideas from other ideas—not
in the trivial notion that a word is different from a thing. A
recent German writer reviewing Paul de Man's *Allegories of
Reading*, reacts with justifiable astonishment at the way in
which Saussurean terms are used in phrases such as "the liberating theory of the signifier" or "the arbitrary power play of

[52] Hawkes, *Structuralism and Semiotics*, p. 146.

[53] Vincent B. Leitch, "The Book of Deconstructive Criticism," *Studies in the
Literary Imagination* 12 (1979), p. 22. The full extent of the confusion is
made clear on p. 597 of Leitch's "The Lateral Dance: The Deconstructive
Criticism of J. Hillis Miller," *Critical Inquiry* 6 (1980): "While our words
refer to things, to concepts and emotions, they are not themselves these entities. The lesson of difference makes this clear. Language in the (prison) house
is differential as well as referential." Did we really need "the lesson of difference" to teach us that words "are not themselves these entities?" Note, too,
that Leitch treats the differentiation that is basic to language—Saussure's
counter to the idea of reference—as if it dealt only with this trivial difference
between words and things while actually *retaining* the idea of reference itself
virtually intact. In other words, while trying to expound Saussure's novel
idea, Leitch commits himself to the primitive idea of meaning that Saussure's
notion is designed to reject and replace.

the signifier" or the "liberation of the signifier from the signified" and insists that these usages are "so verbreitet sie auch
neuerdings sein mögen, sprachtheoretische Unbegriffe. Zu
Unrecht beruft man sich dabei auf de Saussure" (No matter
how widespread these are, they are nonsense-concepts in the
theory of language. It is wrong to appeal to Saussure in using
them).[54] Other equally incoherent but also widespread assertions are, for example, that "sign and meaning can never
coincide"[55] or that "language is more than meaning." Such
remarks can not even be wrong—they are, to use Kurz's term,
more *Unbegriffe*. For since meaning is an aspect of a sign, can
it mean anything to say that sign and meaning do not coincide? And since language is a system of signs, what can it mean
to say that language is more than meaning? Of course, one
understands the intent of these phrases, an intent to support
and elaborate the view of meaning discussed earlier in this
chapter. But a judgment of the coherence of this use of terms
in the theory of language is quite another matter.

What, then, are the results of this discussion of Derrida's
ideas on language and meaning? Derrida's major thrust lies in
(1) an attack on the essentialist view of meaning typified in
logical positivism, for example, but also found in Platonism
and many other sources and (2) the development of ideas that
run counter to that view. Neither of these two aspects of his
work is successful. The first fails because Derrida allows it to
become embroiled in an unnecessary and fallacious argument
about the priority of writing and speech; because it lacks the

---

[54] Gerhard Kurz, *Arbitrium* 1 (1985), p. 11. Kurz continues aptly, "Diese
[i.e., Saussure's] These enthält keineswegs die Lizenz, den Signifikanten vom
Signifikat lösen zu können. Sprachliche Zeichen ohne Bedeutung sind keine.
Die 'liberating theory of the signifier' missversteht, was bei de Saussure als
eine epistemologische Trennung gedacht war, als eine ontologische und sub-
stantielle" ("Saussure's thesis in no way involves the freedom to divorce the
signifier from the signified. Linguistic signs without meaning do not exist. The
'liberating theory of the signifier' erroneously understands what for Saussure
was an epistemological distinction as an ontological, substantial one"). This
last sentence puts the basic logical error of deconstruction's handling of Saussure's theory of the sign very neatly.

[55] Paul de Man, *Blindness and Insight*, 2d ed. (Minneapolis, 1983), p. 17.

perspective of the many other prior attacks on this theory and thus does not learn from and build on them; and because it is incoherently formulated. The second fails because its key points are not supported but simply asserted, which means that many obvious logical difficulties are ignored and equally obvious objections are not met by any argument; because while using the terminology developed by Saussure, Derrida misuses those terms without explaining why he is doing so and possibly without understanding that he is garbling them; and because the very heavy emphasis on iconoclastic denunciation of logocentrism, now surely unnecessary, prevents Derrida from facing the real task he had to face—developing an alternative, not to logocentrism, but to the alternatives that have already been developed by thinkers that he does not consider.

Derrida's rejection of logocentrism is not revolutionary, and because he thinks it is, he is unable to take advantage of the sophistication that the debate on essentialist thinking has already reached; as a result, he jumps from one extreme (meaning is a matter of fixed, immutable concepts) to the other (meaning is a matter of the indeterminate, infinite play of signs). This appears very like the undeveloped response of one who has just been surprised by the realization that real essences do not exist. The conclusion of this discussion can therefore only be that Derrida's contribution to the debate on language and meaning is not substantial; it fails to establish any coherent new view of meaning or of the way language functions. Still, these ideas have achieved considerable currency in literary criticism. How and why, with what justification, and with what results is the concern of the following chapters.

CHAPTER THREE

Deconstruction and the Theory and Practice of Criticism

M OVING FROM DERRIDA'S IDEAS on language to the phenomenon of deconstruction in criticism is not a simple matter: it is not just a matter of a particular view of language being incorporated into and influencing criticism. There are, for example, two major strands in deconstructive criticism, but of these, the one that derives more directly from Derrida's view of the nature of signification—the limitless, infinite, indeterminate play of signifiers—is less important than the other, which derives more from Derrida's temperament, habits of thought, and style. For the second, Derrida's habit of looking for and denouncing unexamined assumptions, his vocabulary of "putting in question" and "problematizing," and his temperamental addiction to provocative statements are most influential. The first strand, then, derives from Derrida's ideas on language; the second, on the other hand, derives from the habits of thought that operated to generate those ideas. The two resulting positions in criticism are actually not logically consistent with each other, as we shall see; but for the moment, this chapter will be concerned with the more important of these strands—the second—the first being reserved for chapter five.

In the preceding chapter, I was more specifically concerned with Derrida's actual position; but my discussion must now deal more broadly with the general phenomenon of deconstructive criticism and with what is happening as a result of Derrida's influence on criticism in the English-speaking world. Whether this criticism is really true to Derrida's work, or reflects a "correct" understanding of him, is a complex matter, if only because of the two contradictory strands in deconstructive criticism that I have mentioned; but for the moment I want to set this consideration aside and examine the coherence and usefulness of the tendencies in criticism that arise from Derrida's influence.

To avoid the danger of inaccuracy or reductiveness that paraphrase may entail, it is as well to make sure that any exposition is conducted only in the words of committed advocates; and since it would still be incautious to rely on any single formulation, it is also advisable to cite the position I propose to discuss in a number of formulations, all commonly thought to be by advocates or sympathizers in good standing.[1] This collection of statements, then, should prove a sufficient basis for discussion:

> Deconstructive discourse, in criticism, in philosophy, or in poetry itself, undermines the referential status of the language being deconstructed.

> As a mode of textual theory and analysis, contemporary *deconstruction* subverts almost everything in the tradition, putting in question received ideas of the sign and language, the text, the context, the author, the reader, the role of history, the work of interpretation, and the forms of critical writing.

> Sooner or later, we learn, deconstruction turns on every critical reading or theoretical construction. When a decision is made, when authority emerges, when theory or criticism operate, then deconstruction questions. . . . As soon as it does so it becomes subversive. . . . Ultimately, deconstruction effects revision of traditional thinking.

[1] These passages are from the following sources: (*a*) J. Hillis Miller, "Deconstructing the Deconstructors," *Diacritics* 5 (1975), p. 30; (*b*) Vincent B. Leitch, *Deconstructive Criticism* (New York, 1983), p. ix; (*c*) Leitch (paraphrasing an interview by Derrida) in *Deconstructive Criticism*, p. 261; (*d*) Barbara Johnson, "Nothing Fails Like Success," *SCE Reports* 8 (Fall 1980), p. 11; (*e*) Jonathan Culler, *On Deconstruction* (Ithaca, 1982), p. 86; (*f*) Leitch, "The Book of Deconstructive Criticism," *Studies in the Literary Imagination* 12 (1979), pp. 24–25; (*g*) Jerry Aline Flieger, "The Art of Being Taken by Surprise," *SCE Reports* 8 (1980), p. 57; (*h*) Christopher Norris, *Deconstruction: Theory and Practice* (London and New York, 1982), p. vii.

[Deconstruction] undoes the very comforts of mastery and consensus that underlie the illusion that objectivity is situated somewhere outside the self.

To deconstruct a discourse is to show how it undermines the philosophy it asserts.

A deconstruction, then, shows the text resolutely refusing to offer any privileged reading. . . . [D]econstructive criticism clearly transgresses the limits established by traditional criticism.

The clearest distinction between traditionalist and deconstructive logic resides in the difference in their attitude toward the exercise of power . . . [and] the abdication of the power to dictate taste.

Deconstruction is the active antithesis of everything that criticism ought to be if one accepts its traditional values and concepts.

These passages vary in emphasis and terminology, but common to all is a pair of elements. First, deconstruction performs an operation that is variously described as undermining, subverting, exposing, undoing, transgressing, or demystifying; and it performs that operation on something variously thought of as traditional ideas, traditional limits, traditional logic, authoritative readings, privileged readings, illusions of objectivity, mastery or consensus, the referential meaning of a text, or simply what the text asserts or says.

My purpose in what follows is to analyze the substance and value of this program as a contribution to theory of criticism. It is necessary, first of all, to distinguish a theory of criticism, on the one hand, from helpful advice, on the other. If, for example, this program is construed as warning us to be wary of received opinion, not to accept traditional views unquestioningly, not to swallow the obvious without looking at subtleties that it may conceal, not to let authority in any field of inquiry intimidate us and inhibit our own thinking things through for ourselves—then this may be good, helpful advice, but it is not a theoretical position. As such, it would not set forward any position of substance that diagnoses particular errors of any accepted critical procedures. It suggests that one oppose what is currently traditional and obvious but not what is wrong with that or what the characteristic methodological error of the traditional, obvious reading is other than its being obvious and traditional; but that is not a *methodological* error. Moreover, this kind of helpful advice would be neither original nor remarkable: it is the standard advice to the researcher in any field. We can all agree that it is indeed helpful advice and could all also probably concede that we need constant reminding of it. But it is advice, not theory, and commonplace, not original.

This may seem a simple point and not worth belaboring, but the emphasis given in the writings of deconstructionists to the questioning of traditional readings and ideas requires that it be made; to the extent that deconstruction might seek to derive any benefit as an original theoretical position from questioning or undermining tradition *per se*, it would not deserve it and would, in so far, be neither original nor theoretical. Attacking traditionalists and traditional ideas affords feelings of daring and exhilaration, but it was doing so long before the appearance of deconstruction, and what really matters is the *specific content* of each particular attack, not the simple fact of being antitraditionalist. Now, some of the passages I have cited do seem to offer only general advice that authority should be questioned; and even if that advice is given a little more specificity with the notion that traditional readings should be subverted or undermined, it is not obvious that we have here anything that is remarkable. To focus on what is really different about deconstruction we must look at the eventual fate of the traditional (or obvious or referential) idea or reading. It is here that deconstruction and the more familiar model of inquiry part company. For in the mode of inquiry with which we are more familiar, a traditional idea that has, to the satisfaction of the great majority of scholars in that field, been questioned, subverted, undermined, and found wanting is then abandoned, to be replaced—until such time as it, too, meets the same fate—by another. But the deconstructive model of progress is very different. The traditional idea is questioned, subverted, and undermined—and then *retained* in order that we can focus on the act of subversion itself, which, however, does not constitute a final rejection of that idea. This is, moreover, required by deconstruction's logic of "neither/nor and either/or"—that logic does not allow the traditional view simply to be rejected and abandoned.

It might seem rather bizarre not to want to move on to a newer and more adequate idea and consign superseded ideas to history and historians, but deconstruction needs this to be distinctive; if it only recommended that we seek out obvious, but inadequate, ideas and replace them with or incorporate them into more complex ones, it would have no characteristic quality to call its own—it would fail to be either an original or a theoretical position. The same conclusion would hold even if a continuing series of deconstructions were envisaged; to undermine one traditional idea so that it is superseded or absorbed by another and then automatically to attack the resulting more complex idea in the same way (since *it* is now the accepted standard idea) is still only the way of research that everyone accepts as normal procedure. Deconstruction does and must then require that the traditional idea be held still and allow itself to be deconstructed *and* retained; and the whole resulting *complex* is the result of the deconstructive method. Since deconstruction wants to show that the text says the opposite (or also says the opposite) of what it seems to say or is traditionally thought to say, the traditional version is the reference point that deconstruction needs both during and *after* it has done its work in order to exist.

There is another way in which the deconstructive program for reading and interpreting literary texts is often stated in more defensible and plausible terms, again at the cost of surrendering its distinctive character and merging with any good criticism—that is, ceasing to be deconstruction. On occasion, deconstruction is defended as a mode of reading that pays attention not only to the surface but also to concealed subtleties beneath it, so producing an interpretation that does justice to the different levels at which a text operates. These different levels may even run counter to each other, so that there is a tension between them: to use the language of an exponent, there are then "warring forces of signification."[2] But anyone familiar with criticism over the last half century will quickly see that we are now very close to a generalized description of what good, alert criticism has been doing for a long time. Indeed, one of the standard procedures of the New Critics was to show how the obvious surface characteristics of a text (plot, major events, explicit themes) could be complicated by textual detail (imagery, metaphor, etc.) that ran counter to the text's more obvious surface content; the resulting tensions and incongruities then required a more inclusive and complex interpretation embracing all levels.

Jonathan Culler is the expositor of deconstruction who is most inclined to expositions that downplay or omit the more dramatic, extreme sides of deconstructive positions in order to make them seem more plausible, comprehensible, and palatable to a wider public, and inevitably his account of deconstructive criticism finds itself facing this difficulty of potentially merging with good criticism generally. How then does he deal with this danger?[3] Culler's attempt to preserve the distinctive identity of deconstructive criticism identifies the traditional version of multileveled criticism as showing "a willingness to celebrate ambiguity," as opposed to which "deconstructive readings may thus refuse to make aesthetic richness an end." But this argument is only able to preserve deconstruction's separate, unique status and value by caricaturing the content of prior criticism. The overwhelming majority of critics who have dealt with different layers of meaning in a text have of course done so for cognitive reasons; and Culler's distinction breaks down as soon as we abandon the fiction that prior criticism was only concerned with aesthetic richness. Later, Culler tries another variant of this argument: "Though deconstructive analyses draw heavily upon prior

---

[2] Barbara Johnson, *The Critical Difference* (Baltimore, 1980), p. 5.

[3] The two attempts cited are on p. 240 and p. 268 respectively of his *On Deconstruction*.

readings and may diverge strikingly from those readings, they may treat these readings less as external accidents or deviations to be rejected than as manifestations or displacements of important forces within the work." But traditional criticism, too, "may" (often does?) treat prior interpretation as incomplete rather than simply mistaken and without any important relationship to the text; in other words, the prior interpretation responds to one aspect or level of the text and so is absorbed into a more complex one. It is, in fact, a critical commonplace that each interpreter learns something about the text even from interpretations he rejects. Culler's deconstructive use of prior readings, then, relies again on an illegitimately reduced account of the general critical use of those readings to make his contrast; when a more realistic account of general critical procedure is used, his contrast disappears.

The really distinctive features of deconstructive criticism are found, not here, but instead in those aspects that Culler tends to shy away from.[4] For if deconstruction is not to merge with a more general sophisticated practice of textual interpretation, we must keep in view what is really distinctive about it, that is, its more radical, categorical, and dramatic aspects. The categorical aspect requires that *all* texts are subject to deconstruction and that *all* language covertly undermines what it asserts. (If we say only that a text *often* works on different levels then we are back in the province of traditional criticism.) The radical aspect requires that there is always a uniquely privileged reading, a reading sanctioned by authority and achieved by repression. And the dramatic aspect requires that some "deconstructive violence," as Norris puts it, be done to that reading—it must be undermined, subverted, denounced, opposed, stood on its head. Without the radical aspect, the bland result would be that we should merely be occasionally arguing against commonly held views—again, just the ordinary business of criticism. And without the dramatic aspect, we should

[4] Those of Culler's detractors who claim that he is not faithful to deconstruction's radical nature seem to me justified; though in agreeing with them on this point I would not share their faith in that radical nature but rather Culler's evident unease with it.

73

only be working toward correctives to common views, introducing more complexity into them, even abandoning them in
favor of a new consensus view—once more, all standard critical territory.

We can see this matter more clearly by looking at the variety
of possible conclusions in multilevel analyses of literary texts.
Some New Critical readings tended to begin by diagnosing
discrepancies between the surface meaning and that found on
other levels but ended by resolving the tensions between the
different levels into an overall coherence; others could retain
to the end the sense of discord and irreducible discrepancy,
depending on the particular text. But deconstruction comes
down heavily and univocally on the side of discord and discrepancy as the universal result, whatever the text; and here
the only thing that is new is the element of inflexibility and
prejudgment.

The unique operation envisaged by deconstruction requires,
then, the literal, obvious meaning sanctioned by tradition and
authority, and the operation itself is one of subverting, undermining, and revising while retaining. Now this investment in
a traditional reading and clinging to it after what might have
been its demise is, from a logical standpoint, the oddest feature of deconstruction and one that probably can only be explained by looking at the ultimate origin of deconstructive
ideas; to this I shall return. For the moment, however, I want
to turn away from the question of the inherent value of the
bewildering exercise that is recommended here to focus on the
question of whether it is, in fact, feasible to do it at all.

Deconstruction must work with the traditional, literal, authoritative, superficial, referential meaning and cannot exist
without it.[5] But here two serious problems arise immediately:

1. Does the single, traditional view of a literary work really
exist? My own major field is the study of German
literature, but though the Germans are reputed to be a
conformist people, I have yet to find *the* received

[5] Other adjectives commonly encountered here are repressive, authoritarian, authoritative, authorial, etc.

traditional view of Goethe's *Faust*, of Kleist's *Prinz von Homburg*, of Kafka's *Schloss*. I do not find things very different, however, in the study of English literature. What is the "privileged" reading of *Hamlet*? or of *Moby Dick*? I cannot find one. If it is objected that I am loading the dice by choosing unusually complex great classics, it is easy to reply that a theory that is inapplicable to the most interesting and complex works of literature is not of very much interest. But that would concede more than is necessary: it is not just the great works that are the stumbling block. All that is really needed is to point to the multicolored content of critical journals today, to the extraordinary diversity of critical schools, and the chaos of conflicting interpretations. To anyone who surveys the present critical scene, with its countless different methodologies and ideological commitments, its divergent readings that are Marxist or Freudian, semiotic or stylistic, historical or New Critical, biographical or feminist—to anyone who surveys this extraordinary scene, the notion that there exists a single, privileged reading is unreal. The very ease with which deconstruction could become one more critical position in American criticism shows clearly enough that pluralism is its watchword. What then will deconstructionists do if they cannot locate the much-needed universal reading of repressive conformity and superficiality? Other critics and theorists can manage with the fact that *in some cases* there exists an unsophisticated, common viewpoint that really ought to be exploded and updated. But—yet again—that commonplace position is only open to deconstructionists if they abandon their claim to have a distinctive position that is *not* a commonplace. And there is no distinctive position without the categorical claim that deconstruction operates everywhere; *all*, not merely some, situations must be subject to deconstruction.
2. Does a single, obvious, literal, and referential reading exist and predominate for all or even most literary works?[6]

---

[6] The word *referential* here is evidently used by deconstructionists in this

Surely this, too, is an improbable idea. The trouble here is that there is almost no such thing as a literal reading of a work of literature: all readings are abstractive and interpretive to a greater or lesser degree, and questions raised about the adequacy of readings always concern the *kind and degree of abstraction*. Presumably, a literal reading of *King Lear* would say that it is about a king with three daughters, one of whom he disinherits; and more of the same kind. I know of no reading that sticks to those statements, but to do anything more—to speak of themes or ideas—is no longer to be literal, it is to abstract. Goethe's poem *Auf dem See* ("On the Lake") has provoked a good deal of interpretation (alas, no authoritative one so far), but none of it says that this is about a man in a boat on a lake—every critic known to me interprets that situation thematically, and there the divergence begins. What would be the literal meaning of *Faust*, especially part two? Or of Kafka's *Die Verwandlung*? Has anyone ever thought that it was a "reading" *at all* to say that the latter is about a man who changes into a large bug? All the critics I have ever read talk about what that development means, and no one has ever claimed that his view of it was "literal." To be sure, one critic will sometimes claim that another's reading of a literary text is too literal—but that must be construed as a demand for a more complex abstraction or perhaps a different one; the critic under fire would scarcely be worth

context as no more than an equivalent to "literal," and for this reason my argument treats only the issue of literalness. The issues that should arise specifically from the word *referential* are more properly issues of theory of language, and these have been discussed above, in chapter two. It is worth noting, however, that to postulate a simply referential meaning of a word is entirely inconsistent with both Saussure's theory of language and Derrida's own rewriting of that theory. This is, then, an example of a fairly typical inconsistency; one cannot *both* reject a particular theory of language as inadequate *and* also accept it and use it to describe a surface meaning of a piece of language that must then be transcended. If the theory is inadequate, it is not usable, and the meaning of a word or phrase must then be stated in other terms.

discussing had he not made *some* kind of abstraction already. If deconstruction really needs *the* literal reading to use as the basis for its rejection and subversion, it will have to work with something that will have no currency at all in critical circles—and what would be the point of attacking and subverting something so insignificant?

If we change the focus from the word "literal" to the words "obvious" or "superficial," the case is not much better. Once again, one must remember the difference between a position that embodies normal helpful advice and that which is needed for a distinctive deconstructive position in theory. We can all agree that we should be alert for the possibility that, in some cases, we are the victims of what may look obvious but is really superficial and inadequate in criticism. To distinguish itself from this unremarkable advice, deconstruction must be categorical: this process must occur in all cases. But this obviously fails to account for the variability of experience, for there is a great variety in currently prominent (though, I insist, rarely *authoritative*) readings. Some are superficial, some are complex. In effect, deconstruction requires us to believe that this variety does not exist and thus to abandon our normal practice of differentiating between the many different degrees of superficiality or profundity that we have always experienced. Some readings are obvious, some are not. Some of those that are obvious to some critics seem less obvious to others. Some obvious readings never seem to be challenged, and that could be due to the fact that the texts concerned are not really very complex, but others may be different in this respect. But the deconstructionist cannot admit all of this without disappearing from the scene: he must claim, contrary to all of it, that experience is not variable and that (*a*) there is always an obvious reading and (*b*) it is always inadequate and subject to undermining and reversal. Most critics may like to think that they see very different degrees of sophistication in critical readings; but if the deconstructionist accepts this, he will end up in the same

77

position that everyone else is in—that is, choosing among differing interpretations according to whether they are superficial or complex and finding fault with the former rather than the latter, just as any discriminating critic does. The problem seems to be that, whenever a reasonable program for criticism is described, the deconstructionist must reject it as part of received opinion, for the word reasonable is just a cover for business as usual. His program *must* be provocative, it must undermine and subvert—hence his need to take extreme positions that, though they may occasionally seem to have something in common with reasonable advice for the critic (e.g., "look skeptically at traditional ideas"), must add a sweeping, categorical element in order to achieve his purposes. But each time this happens the result is that his position thereby becomes untenable.

Accompanying the opposition to a "referential" meaning there is often an emphasis on "rhetoricity" or "figurality" as something that fundamentally changes the perception of a text's meaning. This is the mechanism by which, it is said, all texts assert (or also assert) the opposite of what they seem to say. (This is particularly characteristic of Paul de Man's work). But the plausibility and/or distinctiveness of this position can be peeled away in layers. First, to the extent that it takes the stylistic or rhetorical form of an utterance to be part of its content, this position coincides with a well-known and much older view that form and content cannot be separated in literary or in other texts. Second, to the extent that style and rhetoric can sometimes be found to run counter to what seems the surface thrust of an utterance, this position is still not distinctive—this, too, has been observed many times before. But beyond this there can only be the position that "always and everywhere" the "rhetoricity" of a text makes it say the opposite of which it seems to say. And once more, it is this categorical claim, a claim deconstruction is compelled to make to achieve distinctiveness, that is vulnerable to easy disproof by just a single instance—and there are surely many such.

So far, I have argued that deconstruction cannot find the reading it needs to perform its task since (1) there is rarely a single received authoritative opinion on any work of literature and (2) readings that have some currency cannot all be characterized simply as literal and superficial but vary enormously in the degree of their abstractness and complexity. And since the single required literal reading cannot be found, deconstruction cannot even begin. But now let us turn to what deconstructionists would propose to do with that reading if they found it.

Here, it seems to me, is the biggest single failing of deconstruction as a recommendation for critical procedure and the focal point of its failure as a theory of criticism. The deconstructive program involves taking the traditional (obvious, literal, repressive, authoritarian, etc.) view and standing it on its head—subverting, undermining, or opposing it.[7] But, even if

---

[7] It is at this point that the inconsistency between the two deconstructive programs for criticism comes to light. On the one hand, Steven Rendall ("Mus in Pice: Montaigne and Interpretation," *MLN* 94, 1979, pp. 1056–71) likes the idea that there are an infinite number of meanings in literary texts, which, presumably, must remove any special importance from *the* privileged meaning—it takes its place as just one among the infinity, and neither it nor its possible opposite would then be remarkable within the infinity. Moreover, from this standpoint it is the reader's creativity that results in the infinity, not the text itself. But J. Hillis Miller ("Deconstructing the Deconstructors," p. 30) locates meaning in the text itself, not in the reader, for Miller merely discovers—not creates—the fact that the text "says two entirely incompatible things at the same time," that is, the referential meaning and its polar opposite. For Miller, then, interpretation focuses on the two readings—the referential and its opposite; there is no "infinity" of meanings, all indistinguishable from the point of view of a text's content. (The "infinity" or "random" strain in deconstructive criticism is the subject of chapter five.) Miller's recent short programmatic statement in the *New York Times Magazine* ("How Deconstruction Works," *NYTM*, 9 February 1986) makes his preference more explicit still: "In a deconstructionist reading, the two meanings are asymmetrical and irreconcilable, like rhetoric and logic. . . . To identify such an interference in the words is far from implying that the reader is free to make

the points I have just argued were to be set aside and the deconstructive case in these respects conceded, this would still be a seriously limited plan for progress in thought and interpretation: for the relationship between a received opinion and a newer view that challenges it is rarely one of simple opposition.

If traditional views in criticism or any other field could be superseded simply by turning them on their head and saying the opposite (whether one then keeps both or simply discards the first), how simple inquiry would be. In the real world of inquiry, undermining and overturning a traditional view happens because a more defensible one is set up to replace it, and there is no knowing where that new view will be found or in what direction one may have to go to find it. Instead of standing conveniently opposite to the traditional view, so that all one has to do is to turn around to find it, the creative new view may be close to it or miles away, to the left or to the right, or simply nowhere in relation to that older position. A newer view may involve modifying part or rejecting the whole, reassembling older parts in new relations to each other and with different emphasis or starting from scratch, seeing a small subtle flaw that vitiates everything in the dominant viewpoint or flatly rejecting a large part of it while still leaving others intact. In short, traditional views can be found wanting for a thousand different reasons and in a thousand different ways.

Here, then, is deconstruction's most significant weakness as a prescription for critical procedure. The focus of any genuinely new piece of criticism or interpretation must be on the creative act of *finding* the new, but deconstruction puts the matter the other way around: its emphasis is on debunking the old. But aside from the fact that this program is inherently uninteresting, it is, in fact, not at all clear that it is possible; for as Charles Saunders Peirce argued against Descartes's recommendation that we should doubt all that we know, doubt can only really arise from *specific* causes and anxieties, not

---

the phrase mean anything he or she likes." Miller here commits himself firmly to a rejection of the alternative strain in deconstructive criticism.

from the contemplation of the present state of knowledge taken only by itself. To find a better, more complex interpretation needs skill, imagination, and thought: it is not at all easy, and the direction in which one must go is not at all obvious. But to recognize this is to see both what the appeal of deconstruction is and why it is fruitless: deconstruction makes the next step easy but trivial.[8] One looks mechanically in the opposite direction. Deconstruction's strategy seems focused but is really random.

To return to the point that I made above, all interpretation is abstraction. But abstraction can occur in a limitless number of ways, which means that fundamentally different abstractions giving greater or lesser weight to different textual features do not differ from each other in one dimension but in any number; if one were to decide to focus on one particular abstraction (say, a traditional one) and its opposite, one would have ruled out the search for all other kinds of abstractions. That being the case, the only way in which deconstruction could work would be if, hypothetically, all traditional views had made the right kinds of abstractions the wrong way round—such an implausible hypothesis that it can immediately be dismissed. Paradoxically, it would seem that deconstruction is a victim of the restrictive binary logic that it likes to denigrate: it thinks in terms of subverting and undermining traditional views, but that excludes the really progressive possibility of just *departing* from those views, their emphases, and their terms. It is surely that kind of departure that provides real progress.

There is, moreover, something extraordinarily conservative about this program. Old views are not to be allowed to die and be replaced; they are to retain stage center in order to be debunked for all time. It is as if they are to be left in eternal purgatory instead of being laid to rest to make way for the

---

[8] The point I am making here has nothing to do with the fact that deconstructive writings are generally difficult reading; cf., for example, the case of Paul de Man or of Derrida himself. I am here referring only to the character of the prescription for progress made at this point in the deconstructive scheme.

next generation of ideas. Obsessive denigration of the old is really a poor substitute for finding something new: it will satisfy the emotional needs of the deconstructive program but not any need for intellectual progress.[9] Deconstructionists are obviously persuaded that theirs is a subtle and sophisticated position, but one cannot have subtlety to order, subtlety as a program. Subtlety is inherent in the particular imaginative act of finding a new view that has value; but that act is unique to each particular situation and is not generated by telling everyone to subvert whatever is traditional or obvious.

Ultimately, then, the position that the traditional and obvious must be systematically opposed and deconstructed is vacuous; it is not really a position in critical theory at all, for it tells us nothing about original thinking in criticism and where it may lead us. Logically, it seems to me on a par with the slogan of the younger generation in the 1960s: "Don't trust anyone over thirty!" Both advocate an indiscriminate response to authority that lacks reflectiveness or discrimination. (To be fair, the younger generation of the sixties never thought of this as a *positive* program in its own right, and it was busy thinking up alternative views of war and society that had their own logic.)

What are we then to make of the popularity of this view of criticism? Its appeal is evidently based in part on its being an apparently provocative, revolutionary movement. There is currently widespread dissatisfaction with the state of literary study in the universities, and deconstruction gives both a form to that dissatisfaction and a sense that its adherents are part of a bold move to sweep aside what is conservative and deadening in the scene; and since deconstruction actually deflects

---

[9] The stagnancy and conservatism inherent in this position are also seen by Graff ("Deconstruction as Dogma," p. 416): ". . . the 'conservative' impulse of deconstruction, its suggestion that having put in question our logocentric assumptions, we can pretty much go on behaving as before"; and Crews ("In the Big House of Theory," *New York Review of Books*, 29 May 1986, p. 40): "[Derrida] has no way of arriving at more fruitful ideas than the inherited ones he has doomed himself to deconstruct ad infinitum and thus to retain in a limbo of combined attention and nonassertion."

attention from any real break with the past by giving conservative views a privileged central position that precludes their being abandoned, there is no substantial progressive idea in its program that might divide potential followers. And yet, as we have seen, there is much in this aspect of the deconstructive program that must seem peculiarly inappropriate to the American critical scene in which it has taken root; to understand all of this, we must go back to its origins in France. Analysis of the doctrine itself merely brings to the surface its logical inadequacies, but a look at its origins may explain much that would otherwise puzzle the English-speaking observer.

There are two features of the French context of origin that seem relevant: the first relating to the academy and the second to French intellectual life in general. As to the first, an unusual degree of rigidity and conservatism prevailed in French universities in the midsixties when deconstruction emerged. A version of literary history and biography that had gone unchanged since the nineteenth century held complete sway in the field; the theoretical turmoil of the last forty years in England and America had barely touched French higher education. In linguistics, too, Saussure's theory of language had given rise to structural linguistics in England and America but had scarcely made a dent in the old-fashioned historical philology that still dominated the study of language in French universities. (A profound irony here is that, even though Saussure is now quoted everywhere in France, there appears to be no understanding there of the fact that Saussure's work radically altered linguistics in the English-speaking world many decades ago while he was being ignored elsewhere.) This degree of conservatism could not simply be a matter of lagging behind on the time scale; a country that was so far behind had to have a far more determined and dogged attitude to the old ways in the study of language and literature, and France had. Nowhere was conservative literary history and biography more pedantic or ossified, and nowhere was there more conformism in what was taught to university students. There was one truth, and it was contained in Gustave Lanson's literary history of France, which students were required to commit to memory. Any deviation from this basic truth provoked a massive, unified reprisal, and that fact constituted a very real repression of any alternative possibilities.

These circumstances obviously explain one of deconstruction's peculiarities: in France, unlike America, there really *was* a single authoritative traditional opinion on literary texts, and it was administered ruthlessly to all. It was indeed repressive. In this environment the deconstructionist found no difficulty in locating his single, superficial, received opinion to debunk; but while this doubtless explains the importance of received opinion for deconstruction, it also exposes the disturbing fact that what we are dealing with is a somewhat automatic response to a primitive situation, not the complex and sophisticated theory that deconstruction claims to be.

The second feature of the French scene is doubtless related to the first. By long-standing tradition, the French intellectual has defined himself by opposition to the dull-witted bourgeoisie and the official organs of the state (such as the university) that are its expression. As a result, an outstanding characteristic of French intellectualism is an obsessive denigration of the bourgeois and all his manifestations. Leo Bersani has aptly termed this the "arrogant frivolity" of French intellectual life.[10] Arrogant, because the French intellectual defines himself through his feeling of superiority to the common herd in his more sophisticated values and perceptions. Frivolity, because the intellectual never tires of startling and chic new postures to shock and affront the bourgeois in his deadly serious commitment to his old routine.

Here, then, is the origin of deconstruction's other strange feature—the obsession with denigrating the traditional reading for its own sake and the need to keep it alive in order to mock it and run dazzling intellectual rings around it, rather than let it pass into obscurity. The ultimate source of this logically odd feature is surely the traditional predilection of French intellectualism for exposing and ridiculing the naiveté

[10] L. Bersani, "From Bachelard to Barthes," *Partisan Review* 34 (1967), pp. 215–32.

of that unsophisticated fellow, the bourgeois.[11] If the bourgeois is so bovinely earnest, the intellectual counters with playfulness. Intellectual contempt for a stationary target of simplemindedness is the very essence of deconstructive method; but here Derrida only absorbs and continues a traditional style and is neither a leader nor an innovator. Consider, for example, this recent description of his predecessor Barthes; the continuity of attitudes is surely striking: "He detested all forms of authority. . . . His temperament and intellectual style were elegant, abstruse, refined, slightly mandarin. He could be assertive, always in the mode of counter-statement, affirming the inverse of society's accepted dogmas and myths."[12] The coincidence of this description with the deconstructionist program surely gives the game away. Derrida makes theory what in Barthes and French intellectualism generally is simply temperament. But surely this intransigent intellectual elitism is not a flexible but an inflexible position; it is conformist in its following the patterns of thought of orthodox Parisian intellectualism but unconducive to genuinely probing, original thought.

This background, which contributes to the shape of deconstruction and explains its logical weaknesses, should not at the outset have seemed a fruitful one for the emergence of a coherent theory. On the one side, pedantry, rigidity, and conformity; on the other, far too much concern with mocking these qualities in order to seem more intellectually fashionable. But instead of rising above this primitive situation, deconstruction in large measure reflects its intellectual weaknesses.

To recognize part of the origin of deconstruction in these aspects of the French critical scene is to be struck again by its inappropriateness outside that context. Instead of harboring the rigid uniformity of Lanson, America is home to a chaos of competing critical ideologies. Obsessive attack on the superficiality and conformity of received opinion is the opposite of

[11] Ibid., p. 217: "What is generally taken for the French critical spirit is a highly developed taste for attacking intellectual dwarfs."

[12] Peter Brooks, "Savant of Signs," *The New Republic* 3534 (11 November 1982), p. 27.

what might be more useful in that context, which probably needs rather a greater degree of inhibition against the acceptance into this chaos of yet another ideology. American criticism could use more agreement on standards of argument, coherence, and usefulness so that new movements such as deconstruction might be given closer scrutiny before they are imported.

There is, in fact, something logically very odd about this mismatch between a critical theory that in its obsession with conformity could only have arisen in France and its acceptance in America, the pluralistically cheerful accepter of diversity. In one sense, this acceptance is very much in the spirit of America's acceptance of European refugees; in another sense, it might seem contrary to that spirit, since there is here no adequate soil to nourish deconstruction's basic thrust.

That contrast evidently worries some deconstructionists. The rapid institutionalizing of this would-be anti-institutional position is a sign of the fundamental geographical mismatch, and so deconstructionists have been provoked by it to consider how, in the American scene, to preserve the subversive spirit of deconstruction. Barbara Johnson's odd solution is to advocate a willing descent into a state of simple-minded ignorance so that one can experience the shock of deconstruction. She thinks of this as the antidote to our becoming comfortable with deconstruction: "comfortable undecidability needs to be surprised by its own conservatism."[13] But the fundamental shape of what she is suggesting here eludes her: she is really suggesting that deconstructionists continually recreate in their own heads the circumstances of the French origin of deconstruction, and what is really worrying her is that the American scene is not cooperative with deconstruction in the right way—an overtly *un*cooperative way. Certainly, this proposal is incoherent, for it is impossible for anyone to suppress his awareness or knowledge in reacting to literary texts.

But this ineffective attempt to deal with deconstruction's failure to find in America the rigid, monolithic conservatism

[13] "Nothing Fails Like Success," p. 14.

86

of the French intellectual scene points to another fundamental problem: it shows how central and indispensable to the deconstructive program is the sense of being revolutionary and subversive. It is not just that the deconstructive program has the *effect*, in a given climate, of being subversive: that would imply that the program can be described in terms of its substance and *then* that, in a climate of opinion that was sufficiently alien to that substance, the effect would be subversion of the prevailing beliefs in that climate. This more normal, recognizable state of affairs is not what we are dealing with here. Instead of the deconstructive program having subversive effects, its program is subversion *simpliciter*. Shock, revolution, subversion are integral to the program's description—it cannot exist without them, and they *are* its substance. But this is surely a logical confusion: revolutionariness is not a position but an attribute of a position. For example: Marxists have a program for a certain kind of society, and revolution is the effect of that program, the means of getting to the goal. Advocating revolution is not an intelligible thing to do unless one explains what for and with what end in mind.

This logical confusion reminds me of Daniel Boorstin's remark about celebrities in the modern world. Boorstin pointed out that many people are well known throughout our society for their achievements in certain fields—Einstein for physics, Babe Ruth for home runs, etc. But, he said, another class of celebrities had now arisen, and these were well known for being well known. Rather unkindly, he picked Elizabeth Taylor as his example. In this sense, deconstruction's revolutionariness is analogous to Elizabeth Taylor's celebrity. It is revolutionary in being revolutionary; it is antitraditional in being antitraditional. If we ask how Wittgenstein is revolutionary, the answer can be something like this: a theory of language that was inherent in the work of his predecessors was examined and found wanting, and as a result a new one was suggested that asked for fundamental changes in established habits of thought. That is logically similar to saying that Babe Ruth is well known for having hit home runs. But if we ask how deconstruction is revolutionary, we shall get an answer such as it stands received opinions on their heads. And that is no more than a restatement of the question, logically analogous to an answer that states that Elizabeth Taylor is well known because stories about her frequently appear in popular magazines. This analysis corresponds to the reality of deconstruction in the American scene and explains some of its puzzles. What is well known, because deconstructionists say it so often, is that it wishes to be a revolutionary new movement. But it is safe to say that what is much less well known, because its advocates find difficulty in explaining the point, is what it is that is revolutionary about it.

At bottom, then, this particular deconstructive model of criticism is not really a program at all. What plausibility it has as a theory derives largely from its apparently speaking to a broad dissatisfaction with the state of literary studies in the academy generally,[14] but its theoretical content is little more than a reactive response to the theoretically primitive situation in which it arose.

So much for the logical content of this deconstructive model of criticism. But does it have any practical value in the current critical situation? It is sometimes suggested that deconstruction's attack on the traditional is in practice a healthy development in America, whatever its theoretical deficiency, for two reasons; first, it helps to loosen up remaining pockets of old-fashioned literary-historical rigidity, and second, it promotes an awareness that readings of literature should look deeper than they have done into the hidden subtleties of texts. I must confess that I am always doubtful of the practical advantages of unsound ideas; they are usually impressive only if

[14] I cannot give an adequate account of this dissatisfaction here, because, while dissatisfaction itself is pervasive, the kinds of dissatisfaction and analyses of the present scene on which each rests are extremely varied. For example, the general dissatisfaction expressed by Harold Bloom in the account by Colin Campbell of an interview with him ("The Tyranny of the Yale Critics," *New York Times Magazine*, 9 February 1986) is quite different from that of Geoffrey Hartman's *Criticism in the Wilderness* (Yale, 1980), while both are a long way from the kind of sense of crisis in William Cain's *The Crisis in Criticism: Theory, Literature, and Reform in English Studies* (Baltimore and London, 1984) or Gerald Graff's *Literature Against Itself* (Chicago, 1979).

one ignores the practical disadvantages that must of necessity flow from anything that is inherently incoherent. Indeed, the net result of the good and bad effects of deconstruction in the present situation seems to me clearly on the minus side.

In general, any wild and incoherent attack on conservatism always tends to strengthen it and to give it added legitimacy. Instead of slowly changing and relaxing with the passage of time, it is suddenly given new life as the legitimate alternative to the current excesses. But in the case of deconstruction, there are added reasons to believe that it promotes rather than erodes conservatism.[15] For, as we have seen, when deconstruction puts such heavy emphasis on the undermining of the traditional view, it is giving that view a privileged status, a permanent existence at stage center where it is to *stay* while being deconstructed. The real way forward from a conservative viewpoint that needs revision is to *go on* from it—to find something better, and that something will not just oppose the older view but replace it. Finding something better is a genuinely progressive move; running rings around a dying idea is neither original nor productive. Deconstruction and conservatism are in a kind of symbiosis in which the two feed on each other; and thus ideas that deserve to die will not be allowed to do so.

The temper of deconstructionist criticism is, in fact, remarkable for its conformism, rather than the reverse; deconstructive writings tend to go over the same ground and use the same vocabulary (logocentrism, difference, demystifying, etc.) without substantial modification or fresh analysis on each occasion. These are not the signs of a genuinely open, intellectually probing new movement.

[15] Cain argues for the same conclusion in a different way in his "Deconstruction in America: The Recent Literary Criticism of J. Hillis Miller," *College English* 41 (1979). For example: "Miller's shift of allegiances to 'deconstruction' ... retains many of the ideas that it appears vigorously to challenge. ... as Miller presents it, 'deconstruction' also reveals a tendency to over-rate the degree of innovation that it introduces to literary studies, and a failure to perceive the conservative impulses that keep its subversive force in check" (p. 368).

89

What of the possible beneficial effects of encouraging a closer look at texts, even if that is only helpful advice, not theory? Again, I am doubtful. As it happens, in 1963 I began a series of studies on Kleist that might superficially seem to be instances of the deconstructive program to come.[16] In writing of Kleist's *Der Zweikampf*, for example, I concluded that "we cannot of course ignore the interpretation of the story that seems to be there at its surface level . . . yet neither can we ignore another interpretation that offers itself as persistently throughout the story." The surface interpretation of the plot outline is an optimistic one, but all kinds of details of the story's verbal texture suggest the opposite, a highly pessimistic account. Well, you may say, if I have argued in this way myself, why should I object to deconstructive criticism? But to say this would be to miss the point entirely. My argument was that this structure of meaning is a distinctive feature of this particular text by this particular author. If it is true by definition for *every* text by every author, my argument is annihilated. A particular view of a text, justified by appeal to its particular characteristics and useful (if it is useful at all) as a particular perception and act of critical judgment, would now be relegated to the status of a routine performance and a routine judgment having nothing to do with Kleist at all.[17] I should have liked my view of Kleist's *Zweikampf* to be considered as a possible reading by others who have read it differently and had hoped to persuade them that Kleist's text did indeed allow and even require this reorientation. But if it is just one more deconstructive reading, it can be ignored by all those who are not persuaded by deconstruction as just another random exercise of the method. I wished to make a point about *Kleist*; deconstruction does not allow me to do so.

The point is that one cannot reach such readings by a me-

---

[16] These were gathered in my book *Heinrich von Kleist: Studies in the Character and Meaning of His Writings* (Chapel Hill, 1979).

[17] Cf. Graff, "Deconstruction as Dogma," p. 415: "De Man's interesting point about Rousseau's writings . . . loses its impact if this discrepancy is known in advance to be inscribed within all writing. What is presumably true of all texts goes without saying for any one."

chanical application of a predetermined approach to all texts; criticism means discrimination, seeing what is characteristic of this rather than that text. Like a stopped clock, deconstruction may on occasion look right, but the fact that it indiscriminately announces that the same result is the right one everywhere, any time, can only lead in one direction: like the clock, it will be easy to ignore. To discover discrepant levels in a text is a *result* of a particular critical investigation; but deconstruction makes it a universally applicable *method*, and that is the logical basis of its error.

And while the attack on some shibboleths of criticism may be welcome, in many cases it will not. Deconstruction has evidently become popular in some measure because of its seeming to encourage and legitimize "the ironic reading" (that is, the reading emphasizing underlying irony) of a text. Doubtless, there are many cases in which this is perfectly justifiable—where, for example, texts that are subtly ironic have been read with wooden superficiality, the irony missed, and the resulting view of the text misses its whole point. (If I am correct, Kleist's work is such a case.) But imagine what happens if we commit ourselves to the ironic reading in *all* cases, indiscriminately. The first result is that irony loses its meaning. If everything is ironic, there is nothing left to give irony its distinctive quality—there is no irony. And the practical results will not always be so attractive either. Shall we have to believe that Hitler is really a hero? That *Troilus and Cressida* is really Shakespeare in buoyant, happy mood? I leave it to the reader to find his own example. *Judgment* is needed in each case—not indiscriminate commitment to reversal and irony.

As a program for criticism, then, this version of deconstructive criticism is vacuous in theory and counterproductive in practice. To oppose a particular tradition or viewpoint with a particular alternative program is to set out a real position; but to announce simply an indiscriminate and unspecified opposition to any tradition in general and none in particular, with no particular alternative in mind in any given case, is not to take a position at all but only to gain rather too easily acquired feelings of iconoclastic superiority. Thinking about real problems is thus circumvented.

THE MAJOR FOCUS of this study is on deconstruction in criticism, since it is considerably more influential in that field than in any other. It is, however, worth noting that the critical position considered in this chapter is structurally very similar to the most general deconstructive way of approaching broader social and philosophical issues; and since the arguments required to analyse this general deconstructive stance are therefore similar to those that I have already used in this chapter, it will be convenient briefly to consider it here.

A recent exposition by a deconstructionist explains that "deconstruction works to show that what had previously been thought marginal may be seen as central, when seen from another position. But this reversal, attributing importance to the marginal, does not lead simply to the reconstitution of a new center, but to the subversion of such distinctions between essential and inessential, universal and particular. What is a center, if the marginal can become central?"[18]

The issue here is a basic and important one in any activity and in any branch or knowledge. Any intellectual pursuit requires, as the first order of business, judgments of what is most relevant to it and what is least relevant. The world presents us with limitless numbers of things and aspects of things to consider—a complexity that is unmanageable until we begin to narrow it down with judgments of what is relevant to our undertaking. But what if our initial judgments of priority and of relative importance are mistaken and result in the exclusion of material that is, in fact, important? That is the possibility on which deconstruction now focuses. In characteristic fashion, deconstruction identifies the center as prescribed by authority and tradition, and the excluded elements as repressed or suppressed, so that the problem is given a kind of moral and political dimension: and so this becomes not simply a matter of

[18] Sara E. Melzer, review of *The Post Card*, by Jacques Derrida, *Los Angeles Times*, 12 July 1987, p. 6.

intellectual error or inadequate understanding but rather one of the tyranny of an establishment's structure of thought seeking to preserve itself by means of its power and authority. But with or without this added factor, the problem of judgments of relevance and centrality is a profoundly important one in any inquiry.

What are we to make of deconstruction's contribution to the understanding of this problem? Once again, the result of a closer look at this contribution is that it evaporates: much less is really being said than appears to be the case. There is, first of all, a "weak" interpretation of it that is similar to that which we saw earlier in this chapter: if what is being said here is that we should all be careful to stay alert to the possibility that our initial setting of priorities and standards of relevancy to any given issue may sometimes inadvertently have excluded things that were in reality central to it, then that is helpful advice and indeed the kind of advice that we all need reminding of often. But it is familiar, even routine advice; it is not theory, nor is it startling or original. A "stronger" interpretation of deconstruction's position here is necessary to justify the notion that this is a distinctive and important program. But the problem is that any stronger interpretations quickly become incoherent.

The "weaker" interpretation set out above is, in any case, obviously inconsistent with the deconstructive position in one important respect, so that a "stronger" interpretation is unavoidable. A previously neglected (or marginalized) element will clearly fare differently in the two cases. In the case that we are more familiar with, we assign to the neglected element a higher priority as soon as we recognize its importance: to use deconstructive terminology, it now becomes part of the center, or "leads to the reconstitution of a new center." Deconstruction, on the other hand, uses this new insight for "the subversion of such distinctions between essential and inessential" and to call in question the very notion of a center, since "what is a center, if the marginal can become central?" But now we have reached the heart of the incoherence in this aspect of the deconstructive program. For here we see the typical distortion that we have seen earlier in this chapter: once again, a received viewpoint is set against an antiestablishment challenger, thus reducing a myriad of possibilities to only two—the traditional view and its polar opposite. To be sure, the distinction between essential and inessential is that of a pair of opposed concepts, which makes it seem plausible to speak as if one could play off one against the other, giving attention now to this one, now to that one of the two. But this conceptual opposition is not represented by two distinct things or sets of ideas in reality: for there we are faced instead with a distinction between the one and the *infinitely* many. Focusing on what is central or essential for a given task or inquiry does not involve a choice between one set of things and another but instead a choice of a small number of things from a forbiddingly large number—in fact, a universe of possibilities. Deconstructionists write as if to subvert this distinction would be to transfer attention from one idea to another; but, in reality, to subvert the distinction between essential and inessential would have considerably more serious consequences. This distinction is one that allows us to focus our minds *instead of letting them wander aimlessly*. Without it we should, in fact, be completely disabled and unable to function intellectually. Without the ability to discern differing degrees of importance and relevance in the potentially infinite variety of things around us, we should be completely lost in a meaningless world.

We can see this clearly enough in our everyday lives: when we find a person who cannot see the forest for the trees, who cannot come to the point in telling a story, or who cannot cut through irrelevant detail to grasp basic issues, we correctly judge that this is a person of limited intellectual capacity. To summarize, then, the weak interpretation of this deconstructive proposal as a suggestion that we keep our criteria of centrality and relevance under constant review is not a theoretical position at all, nor is it an unusual injunction; but the stronger interpretation required to make this not simply helpful advice but a consistent strategy of thought quickly becomes incoherent (1) because the marginal cannot simply refer to a definable idea that can replace another equally definable one but instead speaks to a limitless chaos of possibilities and (2) because to subvert the distinction between essential and inessential (which is not the same thing as saying that its application has gone wrong in a particular case) would be to forbid productive mental activity and the power of abstraction on which it rests.[19]

There are, in fact, grounds for concluding that this aspect of the deconstructive program is, from a logical point of view, vacuous: that is, it may seem to be saying something but really is not. Imagine a conference on cancer research at which the general sense is that recent research is going nowhere. A deconstructionist rises to tell the conference that it must look at hitherto marginalized, thus neglected, ideas. A researcher, intrigued by the possibility of a new idea, asks what specific suggestion or suggestions the deconstructionist has in mind. But the deconstructionist replies only that the field must question its concept of what is central to cancer research. Evidently, replies the researcher, but just what aspect of the current consensus on centrality is the problem, and which of the thousands of currently neglected chemical possibilities is the one that the deconstructionist is recommending? If now the deconstructionist replies that he is recommending a general strategy, not a concrete proposal, the audience will conclude, correctly,

[19] In practice, of course, deconstructionists find the distinction between essential and inessential just as indispensable as everyone else does; neither its existence as a distinction nor its utility is put in question by Melzer's actual procedure in the passage with which I began this discussion, for there, without acknowledging as much, she is clearly summarizing and thus giving the essentials of a passage by Culler: "On the one hand, the marginal graft works within these terms to reverse a hierarchy, to show that what had previously been thought marginal is in fact central. But on the other hand, that reversal, attributing importance to the marginal, is usually conducted in such a way that it does not lead simply to the identification of a new center (as would, for example, the claim that the truly important thing about *The Critique of Judgment* is the attempt to relate different kinds of pleasure to the inside and the outside of the work of art), but to the subversion of the distinctions between essential and inessential, inside and outside. What is a center if the marginal can become central?" (*On Deconstruction*, p. 140).

95

that he has nothing to say after all. For what he has just said is rather like saying, "Have a good new idea." That is not even a strategy for finding new ideas, much less a new idea in itself.

Doubtless, this aspect of deconstruction has gained some credibility from those particular situations where specific perspectives have been neglected: in the deconstructive rhetoric of the marginal becoming central and of subverting the distinction between the two, feminists have seen support for their sense that female voices have been neglected; the same is true of Marxists with regard to voices from outside the political and social elite. But feminists and Marxists are very mistaken to see support for their position in deconstruction's rhetoric. For they are surely attempting to identify *particular* omissions from the center and making *specific* proposals to change the consensus, which is as it should be. But given such aims, deconstruction's generalized strategy is a very dangerous thing: if, as a result of feminist and left-wing efforts, male chauvinist and fascist voices become marginalized, will that very fact make them suddenly intellectually respectable again? Surely that would be an unacceptable development, but it is the conclusion to which we are committed by deconstruction's essentially random theory of the vitality and importance of that which has been marginalized. I take it that the vitality of feminism lies not simply in the fact that it has been a neglected perspective (that would not distinguish it from the perspective of believers in the flatness of the earth) but rather in the fact that it is a neglected perspective that is too inherently valuable to ignore. The center that ignored a female perspective was a defective center specifically to the extent that it ignored that perspective. But this conclusion is the result of a particular judgment on a particular set of circumstances; it cannot result from a general strategy of reversing the central and the marginal because that strategy would actually prohibit such judgments. In deconstruction's general strategy, it is marginality that is the issue, not the inherent value of some rather than other marginal elements.

CHAPTER FOUR

What Does It Mean to Say That All Interpretation Is Misinterpretation?

LARGELY IN THE CONTEXT of the views I have been dis-cussing so far (though by no means completely so, since Harold Bloom came to it independently),[1] a new view of the nature of interpretation has arisen. Interpretation is a central issue in the humanities, and the logical status of interpretation has been and always will be a correspondingly important issue in the theory of criticism. When a radically new view of its nature is advanced and the theoretical debate to that extent enlarged and enriched, something noteworthy has happened. The recent appearance of the view that "all interpretation is misinterpretation" might seem to be such an event. The purpose of this chapter is to clarify just what it is that has happened.

By now, the view that all interpretation is misinterpretation, and all reading misreading, has been around long enough to have been debated—and attacked—a good deal. One might have expected the debate to have clarified the nature of the new position; but that has not happened. If I am correct, no progress has been made because opponents have been so offended by it that they have immediately positioned themselves to show that it was incorrect before giving attention to the possibility that its being correct or incorrect was not really the issue. There is, in fact, a much more important and ultimately simpler judgment of what this new position contributes to the debate than the judgment that it is erroneous.

Something odd can be seen just in the responses of propo-

---

[1] Harold Bloom, a leading advocate of this view of interpretation, though allied with deconstructive critics, is also an independent figure who reaches this position by his own path; cf. his *The Anxiety of Influence: A Theory of Poetry* (Oxford, 1973) and *A Map of Misreading* (Oxford, 1975).

nents to the attacks on their position: they seem almost to be delighted by those attacks. It is as if the attacks themselves were necessary in order for their position to be completed and its force to emerge. What generally happens is this: opponents have a strong intuitive conviction of the foolishness of the new thesis and therefore attack it with a directness that corresponds to the strength of that conviction. The resulting argument is usually based on an appeal to a commonsense feeling that this is an absurd and obviously wrong position. But that is what so delights those who like this new view: they have lured their opposition into taking the very position they need them to be in—the apparently solid and square, but actually naive and unthinking, ground of common sense that refuses to question habitual thinking. The naive defender of the status quo is, in fact, the proponents' favorite target; the appeal to common sense and to obviousness thus brings forth that scorn for and derision of the unthinking that is so important a part of the appeal of "all interpretation is misinterpretation."

Take just one example: M. H. Abrams in his essay "The Deconstructive Angel" is obviously thoroughly exasperated with this whole phenomenon and is provoked by it to say, "[T]he historian is indeed for the most part able to interpret not only what the passages he cites might mean now, but also what their writers meant when they wrote them. . . . [I]f it is sound, this interpretation approximates, closely enough for the purpose at hand, what the author means."[2] And so Abrams presents the deconstructionist with his favorite target: the man who claims to know the truth. It then becomes easy for Abrams's opponents to round out their argument and let it achieve its full force. It is, they say, precisely the merit of their new view of interpretation that it will rescue the profession from this kind of rigidity of thought, complacency, and closed-mindedness. Even a somewhat more guarded version of the same attack can be treated similarly: the complaint that we can clearly distinguish between better and worse interpretations can be dealt with in the same way, that is, as a claim

[2] *Critical Inquiry* 3 (1977), p. 426.

to have access to at least some, if not all, immutably true facts. Here, too, the great diversity of and disparity between different interpretations (historical, psychological, Marxist, feminist, etc.) of the same work will render it easy for the charge of complacency and naiveté to make an easy hit once more. It is as if we are watching a judo contest. One side provokes the other side into an ill-considered lunge then neatly steps aside and uses the attacker's own momentum to send him sprawling in a heap, where, of course, he still thinks he had every right to have won the argument and wonders what went wrong.

None of this is really very satisfactory from the standpoint of an interest in the logic of the issues; those issues are not illuminated by it. But what did go wrong? One major problem here is that a strong and widely held intuitive belief (even one that turns out to be justifiable) in the inherent unsoundness of an argument does not guarantee that the logical problems of that argument are easy to spot;[3] but that strong intuitive belief nonetheless makes opponents overconfident and therefore careless. It is not, in fact, at all necessary to let the proponents have such an easy time of it.

There are here two important considerations that are commonly ignored and that, if heeded, would seriously change the tenor and direction of the debate. First, when a new theory is put forward, it is necessary, before doing anything else, to look carefully at the logical status of what has been said. Opponents have, in their annoyance with the whole matter, allowed themselves to jump to the conclusion that this new view is wrong before they have adequately considered what there is in the theory that could be wrong; the point is that a theory may lack force for reasons quite other than that it is invalid. And second, a new theory of interpretation that arises in the narrow context of a squabble between critics of literature as to the value of a particular new trend in criticism should, if it is to be properly evaluated, be referred to the much wider context of the long and complex debate over interpretation and

[3] Clear examples of this generalization are provided, for example, by age-old conundrums such as Zeno's paradox.

99

certainty. But in this case, it has generally stayed narrowly situated within a recent, limited context and ignored that wider context.

To relate these two points more particularly to the shortcomings of the recent debate, there is, by now, a very long history and a large written literature on the question of whether clear and certain knowledge is possible such that the clarity of the experience is a guarantee that that knowledge is final and not subject to possible future modification or even abandonment in the light of future discoveries or reinterpretations. For some time now, the most common position in the philosophy of science has been that this cannot be the case and that all knowledge is provisional, waiting for something to come along that may cause it to be rethought. Goethe was among the first to see that everything that seems to be fact is actually infected by the framework and terminology of a theory ("Das Höchste wäre zu begreifen, dass alles Faktische schon Theorie ist")[4] and that the only available criterion of validity is not the psychological conviction of the researcher but the always provisional assent of the community of scientists to the arguments and evidence in favor of the alleged "fact." Charles Sanders Peirce, more than a century ago, saw already that all knowledge was in the nature of a hypothesis, subject to modification and critical reformulation by future experience. And these opinions and many like them have become an entrenched part of the thinking of the learned world.

Viewed against this broader background, a reasonable judgment of the value of the recent debate over the meaning and usefulness of "all interpretation is misinterpretation" will be obvious enough: it is not very well informed and not really very interesting. On the one hand, proponents cannot really be allowed to get away with the claim that they deserve the credit for having gotten rid of absolute truth and objective knowledge. That was really done a very long time ago, and

---

[4] "The most important thing is to understand that everything that is factual is already theory." *Goethes Werke* ("Hamburger Ausgabe"), 10th ed. (Munich, 1982), vol. 12, p. 432.

the resulting epistemological position is not a new and provocative one but instead a commonplace. But their opponents, on the other hand, are just as guilty in unnecessarily offering them this ground to occupy, ground to which they have no claim.

The fact that individuals advance particular ideas with great conviction, or that ideas so put forward find wide and longlasting acceptance, has of course nothing to do with this logical point: at any time, a new idea can arrive and persuade knowledgeable people that it should be accepted in place of a former one. Abrams is himself noted for having done just this, and hence it was unnecessary for him to take the position (obviously due to his impatience with this new view) that there are some things the historian can know, period. But to return to my point that a wider view of the context of this argument was necessary, the judgment that Abrams and others who have attacked the view that "all interpretation is misinterpretation" were incautious and inaccurate in their attacks does not imply that their opponents' response was an appropriate one. From a logical standpoint, that response is also inaccurate and ineffective. A reasonably accurate reply would have been, for example, in something like the following form: "The argument of our detractors is ineffective because it assumes and appeals to certainty in knowledge—an assumption widely held to be dubious." But that is not the characteristic form of the response. Instead, it is more like this: "Our detractors have shown precisely what it is about our theory that is its chief characteristic and merit: the debunking of absolutes in knowledge."[5] The first might be reasonable, the second is not. It is

[5] I have not used deconstructive jargon here, e.g., "privileged ideas" or "demystify," because to do so would be to concede a crucial part of the issue: it would imply acceptance of the fact that this point is new and has its origin in this language. But these new coinages are completely unnecessary; there were plenty of quite acceptable ordinary English words for the status of entrenched ideas and for the process of questioning and undermining them. The avoidance of this perfectly ordinary, available vocabulary seems to me to be part and parcel of an attempt to create a feeling that something extraordinary and unusual is going on. As my text argues, it is by no means clear that this is really so.

not just that the position claimed here as the unique province of the proponents is, in fact, very unoriginal: the point is, more strongly, that in the study of literature it is the majority view, and in fact a commonplace, that certainty is not available. The most widely accepted view in criticism is that there are many different approaches to literature (historical, critical, psychological, etc.) and that all shed light, no one being absolute and exhaustive.[6]

What does happen, then, if we (1) look carefully at what is being said before pursuing the question of its validity and (2) set the results in the larger context of the long history of these issues, a much wider one than that of a local political squabble between rivals for critical prestige and power? What does the new view really have to say, and what does it add to the broader debate?

We have already, in effect, rejected one possibility: if "all interpretation is misinterpretation" is simply making the point that there are no absolutes and that there is no special class of unassailable knowledge in criticism, then that is really rather uninteresting. This is a thoroughly familiar position and not the special province of deconstruction; as we have seen, its use as a tactical shot against an opponent who stumbles into a silly stance cannot provide a meaning and a justification for "all interpretation is misinterpretation." Of course, some advocates do state the meaning of the proposition in this way, without noticing that their bold new view has in this formulation become negligible. Jonathan Culler provides an example of this when he explains its meaning as follows: "Since no reading can escape correction, all readings are misreadings."[7] This blindness to the difference between a bold new view and a very ordinary one is precisely the result of a failure to keep one's eye on the broader context and history of the debate that

[6] See the discussion of this issue in my *The Theory of Literary Criticism: A Logical Analysis* (Berkeley, 1974), especially chapters five and six.

[7] Jonathan Culler, *On Deconstruction: Theory and Criticism after Structuralism* (Ithaca, 1982), p. 178. Once more, Culler supplies an eminently reasonable translation of deconstruction into rational language, without noticing that he has destroyed it by doing so.

I mentioned above. That *any* assertion or claim to know something is open to later rethinking is obvious and has long been so; it cannot be used as a new view of interpretation.

If we move to the larger context to see how the new view (or any other theoretical position on interpretation, for that matter) shapes up within that context, we shall essentially be trying to find in it some substantial addition to the theoretical debate on a small complex of questions: What is the logical status of interpretation? What are good reasons for an interpretation? How can we characterize the kinds of evidence that will support an interpretation? And so on. What then does "all interpretation is misinterpretation" add to the debate over any of these questions?

Let us try various possible ways of relating the assertion to these different aspects of the theory of interpretation. First, on the status of interpretation, can the point be to argue that interpretation is not a meaningful activity? Evidently not. Or that no conclusive interpretation is possible? That, as we have seen, is a logically trivial position. There is a variant of this position to consider here, however, that must be mentioned if only because it is thought a highly significant position by its proponents. The argument in question focuses on the origin of the text and the impossibility of recovering the meaning that the text had in the mind of its originator. In this sense, "all interpretation is misinterpretation" denies the possibility of an access to this meaning and so makes the meaning of the origin (the term "originary" is sometimes used here) an unachievable norm.

But the attentive reader will quickly see two ways in which this argument can be judged to add nothing new to the debate: first, it is, as we have already noted, only a variant of the rejection of absolute certainty in any inquiry. *Any* statement about the world can be questioned and is, in theory, subject to rejection or refinement in light of later thought; and to say that the same is true of any statement about the original meaning of a text is only to say that what is true of knowledge in general is true of texts and meanings. The second objection is, perhaps, even more telling. For the view that the intention of the author is neither available nor relevant as a standard of interpretation and judgment has long been familiar in literary criticism as the "intentional fallacy." This classic statement has been the subject of endless debate, and it is puzzling that proponents of "all interpretation is misinterpretation" seem to want to appropriate that position as their own original, bold, new view when it is neither new nor bold.

If we are looking for any new insight into the general logical status of interpretations, then, it seems clear that "all interpretation is misinterpretation" offers neither anything that is new nor even a new facet of anything that is old. Let us turn to the next possible area of contribution to the debate: Does the new view have anything to tell us about the reasons for an interpretation?

Could it be arguing, for example, that there can never be any good reasons for entertaining a particular interpretation? Here we must remember that "good" cannot mean "conclusive" without our being left with the logically trivial position already considered. But "good" can easily mean something more moderate: good reasons are reasons that might seem appropriately supportive of a conclusion, as opposed to reasons that would be judged as specious and irrelevant. Could "all interpretation is misinterpretation" mean that there are no good reasons in this more moderate sense? Well, if so, this would certainly not be a trivial position; but surely it would be absurd, and I doubt that many proponents could accept that this is what they are really saying. If there are never supportive reasons for any interpretation, interpretation is a worthless activity; and so we are back to a previously considered unacceptable position. (If, in fact, a proponent does argue that there are no supportive reasons, it is virtually certain that he does so because he confuses this position with the stronger claim that there are no *conclusively* supportive reasons.) Could it, on the other hand, mean that all reasons for an interpretation are *equally* good and *equally* bad? But that also makes interpretation a worthless activity: surely an absurd result again.

To try once more, could there be anything else in this new

view of interpretation that is trying to deal with the differentiation and evaluation of certain kinds of interpretations or certain kinds of evidence for them? One senses in the writings of proponents an antipathy toward a certain category of interpretations, which might be described as those that are traditional or based on obvious, surface considerations and evidence. Perhaps, then, "all interpretation is misinterpretation" really means that all traditional, obvious, or superficial interpretations should be seen as misinterpretations?

But there would be many reasons to conclude that this is a dubious gloss and that it would only result in an uninteresting position. First, the form of the statement is categorical: "*all* (not just some specified) interpretations are misinterpretations." If the objection is really only to a certain category of interpretations—those that are common—why not say so, instead of misleading with a categorical statement? Why would a theoretical proposition claiming to be an important one omit all of the core information that gives it its actual significance? Second, and even more important, there are no senses of this amended version that are not trivial or dismissable. No one will object to the view that all traditional, conventional views should be given close scrutiny—though, to be sure, one might object to the assertion that an interpretation can be dismissed or declared incomplete *simply because* it is traditional. The real objection here is surely that it is just too easy to express a generalized scorn for all received opinion: much more valuable is the hard work of finding out what is wrong with a particular received view and thinking up a better one. Pouring scorn on received opinion, *in the absence of specific reasons in each case for rejection* (with those reasons then being subject to the same exacting scrutiny that the traditional view received), actually achieves nothing; the achievement of originality lies in carefully looking for hidden inconsistencies in received opinion. But I doubt that anyone who says obsessively that "all received opinion is misinterpretation" will be looking carefully enough, or with enough discrimination, to spot those hidden flaws that everyone else has missed. Any advance in knowledge comes from a search for a specific *new* view, not from the obsession with the categorical inadequacy of old views. Once more we return to the point that the major logical weakness of "all interpretation is misinterpretation" lies in its categorical form.

For the sake of completeness, we must consider one further attempt to supply meaning to "all interpretation is misinterpretation." There is a common attempt to give it further specificity by saying that all interpretation is misinterpretation *because of* the psychology of the interpreter: his needs, preconceptions, and biases come into play to undermine his interpretation, which will therefore involve misinterpretation. But it is only the frequency with which this expansion is encountered that makes it necessary for us to consider it: for it, in fact, says nothing at all about the factors that bear on the evaluation of an interpretation or on the appropriateness of the reasons that may support it or on the ways in which one might judge it incomplete. Instead, this supplementary explanation speaks only of the motivation of the interpreter and of the *reasons for* the limitations of his work; and to say this is to say nothing about how one might diagnose or evaluate the limitations of an interpretation. To be sure, there is an implication that, because of the interpreter's motivational limitations, all interpretations *must* be incomplete in the same sense: but this position once again can quickly be shown to be either trivial or false.

As to the first of these possibilities, it would obviously be trivial to say that all interpreters bring their own preconceptions, biases, and psychological limitations to their interpretations and that these must have an impact on their work to a greater or lesser extent. Who could doubt this? Proponents commonly try to disguise the triviality of this kind of assertion by using a special vocabulary of their own with which to refer to motivation. Instead of the terminology I have used so far—"preconceptions, biases, and psychological limitations"—a very specific language is used that seems intended, through this specificity, to be making a more unique point: for example, "blindness" and "desire" have become particularly fashionable substitutes for the more common vocabulary used to speak of bias or prejudice. But the aura of originality and specificity that is the obvious goal of this special vocabulary cannot change the logical point involved, which is unoriginal and unremarkable.

If any stronger point is being made here, one strong enough to be a genuinely new addition to the debate, it would seem to me that it can only be something like this: "all interpretations are *equally* limited because of their authors' biases (or blindness or desire)" or perhaps "all interpretations are limited in the same ways because of their author's biases." But both of these are patently quite false. Some people handle their biases better, some worse, than others; and different kinds of preconceptions affect interpretations in different ways. That we should all beware of the particular interpreter's biases is doubtless a useful general admonition, then, but not a profound or unusual one, and it is certainly a long way from being important new theory. And to the question "How can we *differentiate* among interpretations by evaluating them to see where bias has done more, and where less, damage?" this new view has nothing to say and nothing to contribute. Once again, it is prevented from being able to contribute to this theoretical question by the grandiose form of the categorical claim: "all interpretation is misinterpretation." For how, given this form, could it contribute to an inquiry that requires distinctions to be made be?

Once more, we reach the same result: the categorical form of the assertion is what dooms it. But this recurring result points to a crucial factor in the situation that cannot be overlooked: it is that the categorical form inherent in beginning with the word "all" is clearly crucial for the psychology of advocates of "all interpretation is misinterpretation." This form involves the exhilaration of a sweeping, bold, unhedged claim. And so it is precisely that feature of the claim that has most psychological value for advocates that renders it ineffective from a theoretical standpoint. Typically, we have found that it is just this form that makes it capable of being construed only in ways that are either trivial or false. For example: either interpretation is never final (trivial) or it is always suspect to the same degree (false); either bias is a constant problem to watch in interpretation (trivial) or bias is always damaging to the same degree or in the same way (false). All the important theoretical issues involved in interpretation require distinguishing one situation from another, i.e., making distinctions between different cases; but the categorical form of "all interpretation is misinterpretation" absolutely and completely excludes it from any discrimination or distinction making and thus from contributing anything to the theory of interpretation.

Surely, the most important judgment of this proposition is not that it is wrong but that it is empty. Its contribution to all areas of the debate as to the nature of interpretation and possible support for a particular interpretation is neither useful nor deleterious, but nonexistent. No intelligent discussion of this alleged new theory is possible because there is no theory.

This result surely explains a very puzzling feature of the situation. Advocates claim implicitly that "all interpretation is misinterpretation" is a very important theoretical statement. And yet, in the debate over its value, advocates and opponents alike have commonly had to gloss it in ways that plainly added a good deal to what was said in its usual formulation. It seems inherently odd, and very unlikely, that what is claimed to be a major theoretical statement could omit so much of its own intended meaning and need so much of its core meaning to be supplied by glosses and explanations. The reason for this is simple: "all interpretation is misinterpretation" has no theoretical content. And that is why no attempt to find a useful meaning for it succeeds.

It was a mistake for Abrams and others to assume that there was a position here to be countered with argument from themselves, and in attacking it, Abrams's mistake compelled *him* to supply a position in order to be able to attack it, thus making it easy for his opponent to dance around him. Not to have any real position to defend is, of course, a great advantage in any argument. If, on the other hand, the advocates of this view were simply asked to explain the point of it, the result would be very different—they would have a much more difficult time of it.

How, then, can we account for the appeal of the view that "all interpretation is misinterpretation"? If I am correct, the impact of this assertion is not difficult to understand when we simply look at a class of comparable assertions that are common enough in everyday life. The proponent of "all interpretation is misinterpretation" does not really have a theoretical position, but he does have something else that is important to him in a different way: a slogan. What is the function of a slogan? Most slogans carry an essentially emotional—not a logical or theoretical—message, and this one is no exception. Slogans are designed not to formulate theories but rather to strike an attitude, to rally a movement, or to intimidate an opposition. This one does all three. I will illuminate the way in which this particular slogan works through an example from a familiar kind of context.

Imagine an everyday kind of discussion, not of interpretation, but instead of the decline of traditional social values and of how and why, for example, delinquency and other social problems are on the rise. Everyone is familiar with the typical attitudes that will be expressed and with the underlying attitudes to responsibility that they represent. Right-wing politicians would blame the courts for not being tough enough in sentencing to provide a real deterrent. Left-wing politicians tend to blame the injustices and immorality of a capitalist society and the disillusion of its have-nots. Parents of teenage children are likely to blame drugs. Political conservatives may blame parental permissiveness and lack of discipline. Social workers might stress poor housing conditions and lack of funding for welfare programs.

A discussion in which all of these viewpoints were represented would find it difficult to reach a consensus, but in theory one might judge that there is at least some small value in each of them and that a discussion of their relative weight was, in principle, worthwhile. All of the factors mentioned are a part of the whole scene under discussion. Presumably, progress in such a debate would consist in weighing the relations between and mutual dependence among all of these factors. (Let us leave aside for the moment the fact that, in the real world, this will rarely occur.) But suppose that a rather self-important clergyman entered such a discussion, exclaiming in ringing tones, "We are all sinners!" Now these same words might be used to good effect by a well-intentioned person to remind those involved in the discussion that there was more than enough blame to go around and that all might well try to understand their own share in that blame instead of blaming everybody else. An intervention of this kind motivated in such a way would, in effect, encourage others to continue their debate and analysis as before, but to do so more thoughtfully and with due regard for their own responsibility. But, in the rather more typical case of the use of these words that I want to consider here, the motivation is different: the self-important cleric has pompously expounded what he thinks is in itself the profound truth that is the key to the discussion. He wants to take center stage and to have the others *stop* their discussion and admire his words.

Perhaps, at first, the others would take his words in the positive sense in which they might have been used, that is, as an appeal to get them to consider their own frailties as well as those of others, and they would go on discussing in this spirit. But this particular cleric interrupts the debate once more to insist on his words *as a position in itself*. Soon all present will see that he is not trying to encourage them to discuss more fruitfully but the reverse; he thinks he has propounded a kind of global view of the situation, an adequate account of it that he wants to substitute for the one they are pursuing. Once they realize this, their attitudes to him will naturally change: they will experience him as a nuisance getting in the way of their discussion. He is simply holding up the debate; he has no interest in pursuing the analysis of how various kinds of responsibility can be diagnosed in the situation and how they function together to create it. Instead, his interest is in grand, categorical statements, whose categorical and undifferentiated form is for him the whole point; any more differentiated and informative statements would not fit his purpose, which is to make a striking and even shocking pronouncement with maximum rhetorical impact on his audience. He is, in effect, uttering a slogan that contributes nothing to the inquiry and impedes its progress by interrupting the real issue-oriented discussion that was going on.

The logic of this situation is very much like that in which the slogan "all interpretation is misinterpretation" is used. If it were used somewhat reticently, and without any aspiration to the status of an actual theoretical position, it could (like "we are all sinners") be interpreted, somewhat charitably, as a gentle reminder to all of us that we should be careful to keep in mind both our own biases and the potential limitations of any interpretation. But if used in a different way, in a manner that attempts to call attention to itself as a powerful theoretical statement in categorical, decisive form, it must be judged as an empty piece of posturing. In neither case is the slogan "wrong," and other participants in the debate will fall into a terrible trap if they mistakenly try to prove that it is. The most logically accurate course, in the case of the advocate of "all interpretation is misinterpretation," as in that of the clergyman, is to go on with the previous discussion and, above all, to make sure that they do not waste the time of those who have a serious interest in continuing to think about the nature of interpretation and of how and whether it can be supported, on the one hand, and about the nature of responsibility and its various different kinds of manifestations, on the other. For the slogan neither makes any real contribution to that debate nor shows any real interest in advancing it; in both cases, the point of its use is surely to draw attention to the speaker through the use of dramatic, categorical assertions that, however, when looked at more closely, say nothing of substance about the issues under discussion. Once again, we arrive at the conclusion that "all interpretation is misinterpretation" is most easily understood if we consider it as a performance. The performance, however, involves principally the massive effect of an apparently large claim, categorical in form, in the grandeur of which proponents may rejoice and be exhilarated, while their opponents are annoyed or intimidated. However, performance often involves illusion, and that is what we have here: an *illusion* of intellectual tour de force, which is not backed up by any theory of substance.

My conclusion, then, is that "all interpretation is misinterpretation" is neither a valid nor an invalid position but no position at all. It merely creates the illusion of a position, and those who believe in that illusion and then try to attack it are hitting empty air; small wonder that they never seem to come off very well in these encounters. The best thing to do with it, so it seems to me, is tell its proponents that we shall all be willing to consider their position on the nature of interpretation when they come up with one; and that, in the meantime, we should devote our energies to studying real, as opposed to illusory, theories.

CHAPTER FIVE

Textuality, the Play of Signs, and the Role of the Reader

I NOTED ABOVE that there were two distinct strands in deconstructive literary criticism, the one being derived more directly from deconstruction's view of meaning as endless signification, the other from its temperamental addiction to challenging and contradicting authority. Some advocates lean more to one, some more to the other, but the two are clearly in conflict. In my third chapter, I dealt with the second of these two possibilities; I want now to turn to the first.

The first thing to be said about this version of deconstructionist criticism is that it is essentially a critical position that can be reached by other routes: for example, its major points are virtually the same as those of the critical viewpoint known as "reader-response" criticism. This convergence is surely explained by the fact that underlying both positions is a very old critical reflex that predates modern formulations of it—the notion that the text is inexhaustible. But the overlap of these different positions has an important practical consequence: deconstruction finds here a supportive environment, since many welcome this aspect of the deconstructive program as added support for a view they were inclined to beforehand. The backdrop of reader-response theory provides a fertile ground for deconstruction and thus adds significantly to its credibility among those whose primary allegiance is not necessarily to deconstruction itself.[1] Because of this practical al-

[1] A position often thought of as allied to reader-response theory is the *Rezeptionsästhetik* developed by a group centered on the University of Konstanz. The most prominent exposition of this position is Wolfgang Iser's *Der implizite Leser* (Munich, 1972), translated as *The Implied Reader* (Baltimore and London, 1974). See also *The Act of Reading* (Baltimore and London, 1978), originally *Der Akt des Lesens* (Munich, 1976). But Iser's position is, in reality, importantly different to the reader-response theory current in Eng-

liance and because the arguments both for and against these
two positions are so similar, I shall deal both with this version
of deconstructive criticism and with reader-response theory at
the same time in the course of my analysis in this chapter. I
find this necessary since not to consider reader-response theory would be not to deal with a major factor in the critical
scene that gives deconstruction a much broader appeal than it
otherwise might have.

A key term in the deconstructive version of this argument is
textuality, and a consideration of this term shows how the deconstructionist train of thought leads to a convergence with
the reader-response viewpoint. One understands this new
coinage best by considering the opposition text/author. We
generally think of the two as linked. Texts result from the activities of authors. Authors are responsible for the existence of
texts. Texts say what authors have made them say; they em-
body a meaning that is the result of an author's decisions to
word them in this way rather than that. The word *textuality*
is introduced to question this entire attitude: instead of depending so much on an author, a text has an independence, a
textuality in its own right. So far, the reader might think that
he sees here the beginning of a more familiar argument, that
concerning the intentional fallacy. But *that* argument, in fact,
moves in a quite different direction: it wants to look for the
meaning of a poem through a careful and thoughtful reading
of it, rather than by consulting its author, because, it is said,
the author may not grasp the full impact of what he has done
in writing something. And this is just a special case of the more
general fact that in any other sphere people may not always
see the significance of their own actions. For that reason, it
may take another person, the critic, working from a perspective that may be broader than the author's, to go further than
he can. But this is *not* the further direction of the argument we
shall be considering; the concept of textuality is a far more
radical idea. In cutting the tie with the author, the implication

---

lish-speaking criticism and for that reason is less relevant to my discussion. It
is also less vulnerable from a logical standpoint.

of textuality is that we cut the tie with *any* idea of a statable meaning; the text now has a life of its own and an endless series of possible meanings, which are no longer subject to control *either* by the author's actions, decisions, and intentions, *or* by the rules and conventions of language. The intentional fallacy questioned only the first, but not the second, of these controlling factors.

Textuality therefore links with Derrida's idea of the play of signs. The signs that make up the text play infinitely against each other, to defeat any possibility of a statable meaning. Attention now shifts to the role of the reader. The view of criticism that we are discussing has abandoned the author and set the text free to mean what it will, but there is no corresponding abandonment of the reader. Textuality is not a concept implying the self-determination of text and independence from *both* authors and readers.[2] On the contrary, readers now take the place of authors. It is readers who are instrumental in the text's myriad meanings coming to light. There is some variability of terminology and formulation of this point. Sometimes the reader is said to *discover* the text's range of meanings, sometimes actually to produce and *create* meanings, but common to all versions of this point is the assertion that the critic is far more important and creative than criticism has assumed him to be. The reader is no longer the humble servant of text and author, and advocates of this view speak scornfully of the false humility of a subservient role for critics and readers of texts: on this point, deconstruction (or at least this strand in deconstruction) and reader-response criticism agree. But once more, to avoid the possibility of distortion by paraphrase, I shall set out some representative formulations of this position by its advocates.[3]

---

[2] This is an important point, since most critics who use the word *textuality* like to think of it as a means of setting the text free, to give the text a life of its own, so to speak. But since this action does not allow for the shape of the text to impose any constraints on its own meaning, it is clear that textuality does *not* mean autonomy and self-determination for the text but instead for the reader.

[3] These passages are from the following sources: (*a*) Steven Rendall, "Mus

CHAPTER FIVE

There is no limit to these meanings since the mind finds in the text whatever it is looking for. . . . The conception of interpretation as a supplement to an integral originary text, often presented as if it were a form of critical humility, is in fact less an exaltation of "literature" than a way of justifying the interpreter's own activity and protecting it from the menace of textuality. By making the text the sign of a sacred presence to which he alone has full access, the interpreter guarantees his own prestige as mediator of the meaning which he invites others to worship as he does. . . . To accept the challenge to interpretation . . . would be to abandon the false humility of critical subordination and embrace the conception of criticism as a form of literature.

What we have here then are two critics with opposing interpretations, each of whom claims the same word as internal and confirming evidence. Clearly they cannot both be right, but just as clearly there is no basis for deciding between them. One cannot appeal to the text, because the text has become an extension of the interpretive disagreement that divides them.

Literature can only be a denunciation of literature, and is not therefore different in essence from criticism. . . . If, as Derrida puts it, linguistic signs refer themselves only to other linguistic signs, if the linguistic reference of words is words, if texts refer to nothing but other texts, then, in Foucault's words, "If interpretation can never accomplish itself, it is simply because there is nothing to interpret."

in Pice: Montaigne and Interpretation," *MLN* 94 (1979), pp. 1057–70; (*b*) Stanley Fish, *Is There a Text in This Class?* (Cambridge, 1980), p. 340; (*c*) Eugenio Donato, "The Two Languages of Criticism," in *The Structuralist Controversy: The Languages of Criticism and the Sciences of Man*, ed. Richard Macksey and Eugenio Donato (Baltimore and London, 1972), pp. 96–97; (*d*) Jane P. Tompkins, "An Introduction to Reader Response Criticism," in *Reader-Response Criticism: From Formalism to Post-Structuralism* (Baltimore and London, 1980), pp. x–xxiii; (*e*) Robert Crosman, "Do Readers Make Meaning?" in *The Reader in the Text: Essays on Audience and Interpretation*, ed. Susan R. Suleiman and Inge Crosman (Princeton, 1980), pp. 151 and 154.

The objectivity of the text is the concept that these essays, whether they intended it or not, eventually destroy. . . . Reading and writing join hands, change places, and finally become distinguishable only as two names for the same activity. . . . Like Culler, he [Fish] believes that giving up the claim to objectivity (which means relinquishing the claim that one knows the truth) is an honest position because it does not pretend to knowledge that is really unavailable.

The statement that "authors make meaning," though not of course untrue, is merely a special case of the more universal truth that readers make meaning. . . . a poem really means whatever any reader seriously believes it to mean. . . . the number of possible meanings of a poem is itself infinite.

As we shall see, it is not difficult to show that this kind of thinking about criticism is based on some rather simple misconceptions, but before proceeding to set them out, let us first consider a simple situation that would immediately make this viewpoint seem implausible. Imagine that a critic writes a critical commentary on Shakespeare's *Hamlet* and another a criticism of Dickens's *David Copperfield*. We should exr ct the results not to look the same. Is the reason for this expuctation the fact that the two works are different or that the two critics are different? Well, suppose that the same critic writes them both. We still expect them to look different. A critic who makes the same remarks about both will scarcely be taken seriously; he will be judged to have ignored the differences between the texts. We expect the two criticisms to look different because *Hamlet* and *David Copperfield* are different, not because the critic wrote them on different days or because two different critics are involved. To be sure, there *are* large problems to be wrestled with in characterizing statements about texts: problems of logic and problems of epistemology. To look at the outline of the situation in the way I have done is not to minimize these problems; it is just to suggest that it is surely very obvious that the solution proposed in the passages set out above must have gone badly wrong somewhere. Where are its logical flaws? There are, in fact, many; let us deal with them one by one:

The "Play" of Signs   As we saw in chapter two, the idea that signs play infinitely and indiscriminately against each other is one that is asserted without any real supporting argument, and it is inherently an impossible one to justify. To be recognizable as *anything*, a sign must have a distinctive shape and function that recognizably sets it apart from other signs. To postulate a sign that simply played indefinitely and infinitely against other signs is to imagine one with no distinct character at all, i.e., one not recognizable as having any shape or function of its own. That produces not more and richer meaning, as advocates of this position like to think, but no meaning at all. A sign not recognizable as anything in particular signifies nothing whatsoever. *Vagueness* in signs introduces diminution, not augmentation, of meaning. Complete vagueness, complete indefiniteness of signification is the point at which zero signification is reached. But not only is this argument erroneous in itself; it is also used by its advocates in the mistaken belief that it is needed to support a particular kind of step in criticism for which it is, in fact, quite unnecessary. It is very commonly used as general theoretical support for a particular critic's finding subtleties and added meaning that had not previously been visible to critics who concentrated too much on the obvious surface meanings of words. But situations such as this do not call for a new theory of signification; all that is needed is to show that previous criticism has been superficial and incomplete in its account of what the text signifies and to offer a more inclusive and complex view of its meaning. Anyone who thinks that this kind of critical move requires a view of signification as infinite and indeterminate is only misdescribing what he has just done: he has not shown infinite meaning but instead additional, *specifically stated* meaning that had been ignored in an inadequate account of the text. The critic has shown something *particular*; he deludes himself if he thinks he has shown something indeterminate and indiscriminate. This is as true of Derrida as anyone else who, when he begins to talk about a text, makes particular assertions and takes specific positions on them; indeed, it could not be otherwise.

Textuality   One of the most important errors of the thinking associated with the word *textuality* lies in the failure to see that there are *two* steps, not one, involved in the notion that a text must be liberated from its author to mean whatever it is taken to mean. There is, first of all, liberation from the author; but second, there is liberation from the rules and conventions of the language it is written in. These are logically separable ideas, requiring separate justification, but the textuality argument always proceeds as if the two were really one and as if a justification for the first were complete justification for both. In effect, the argument operates with just two alternatives: either a text means what its author meant—or we have textuality and free play. And, in so doing, it jumps over an enormous middle ground as if that did not exist. That middle ground, moreover, is already much explored; to ignore it is no longer possible in a competent and knowledgeable treatment of these matters.

It was the argument over the intentional fallacy, as Wimsatt and Beardsley termed it,[4] that first raised doubts about the author's intent as the ultimate appeal in deciding the meaning of a text. But in the forty years since the first appearance of this article, the matter has been discussed at length and further illumined and refined by hundreds of critics and theorists. One of the strangest features of the argument that pronounces the liberation of the text from the author by means of textuality is that it behaves as if this long debate did not exist and as if no one had ever before questioned the author's intent as the touchstone of textual meaning. The problem here is not principally that deconstructionists, in particular, do not see how unoriginal it is to question the role of the author's intention; the major problem is rather that to ignore a large and complex

[4] William K. Wimsatt and Monroe Beardsley, "The Intentional Fallacy," in *The Verbal Icon: Studies in the Meaning of Poetry* (Lexington, 1954).

body of writings devoted to this issue is to enter the situation at a more primitive level than was necessary, by failing to take advantage of prior explorations. For the assumption that to liberate a text from its author is to liberate it from all constraints is a primitive one. It leaps from one extreme to another: total constraint or none at all. Any productive argument should by now have focused on the *kind* of constraints and how they operate. There is one obvious constraint that operates on all texts: the language they are written in. No text in English can escape from the fact that it is in English, not another language. An English text means what it does because it uses the system of communication that is the English language; its meaning is bounded by that constraint; and no theory that denies the need to know how to operate in English and to show a mastery of its conventions in order to understand that text can possibly achieve credibility or command intellectual respect. Total freedom (and textuality if so understood) is therefore an impossible notion.

To consider the meaning of a text as a broader matter than its author's intention has nothing to do with allowing it to mean anything; it simply represents the decision that meaning is best described not in terms of mental processes—which are unobservable and unrecoverable—but in terms of the text's particular use of the linguistic system that it employs.[5] This was the point of the argument about the intentional fallacy; but deconstruction never comes to terms with it, instead returning to the initial step in the argument that began so long ago. But this failing is not an accident: it is the predictable result of deconstruction's habit of reversing a situation, of going from one extreme to another, which here leads it to

[5] The debate sparked by Wimsatt and Beardsley is, of course, only an example from one field; equally relevant here is the much-discussed Wittgensteinian argument about the possibility of a private language, another example of a long exploration of the fruitful middle ground in between the two extremes that deconstruction likes to work with. For a discussion relating Wittgenstein's private language argument to the issues of literary criticism, see my "Wittgensteinian Thinking in Theory of Criticism," *New Literary History* 12 (1981), 437–52.

avoid all the really interesting critical theory on this point of the last four decades.

There is a difference of emphasis here between the deconstructive and reader-response versions of this argument: deconstruction tends to stress more the free play of signs; reader-response, the freedom of the reader's mental processes. But the latter is, if anything, even more vulnerable than the former, for it returns us once more to mental processes and private, unobservable, and unrecoverable facts. Yet it was in large part the unavailability for scrutiny of mental processes that led to the rejection of the author's intent as a touchstone of meaning. Reader-response criticism now makes this problem worse, not better. The initial step of the reader-response argument makes all mental processes arbitrary, so that no mental process has any necessary relation to the text that provokes it. From this it must follow that my meaning has no necessary relation to your meaning.[6] Yet this conclusion so completely ignores the

[6] Stanley Fish is something of an anomaly here, since he has long since committed himself to the initial assertions of reader-response criticism and (as the passage I have cited shows) continues to do so but, by changing his position a number of times, has struggled with the kinds of unacceptable consequences of those assertions that I have set out in this chapter. But his latest reformulation, which is offered as if no more than a refinement, amounts in fact to his abandoning its essentials completely. His most recent version, then, involves the postulation of interpretive communities, with assumptions and conventions that guide interpretation; this, in his view, allows communication to take place and so rescues him from the consequences of earlier formulations. Now it is, of course, true that a text means nothing without conventions shared by the speakers of the language concerned, but to acknowledge this *fully* would, as Fish sees, abolish his reader-response position: if readers are guided by the rules of language, they do not have the freedom envisaged by reader-response theory, and so the text together with its relation to the linguistic system can be the place to which disputes are appealed after all, contrary to the statement by Fish that I cited. In order to continue to cling to his reader-response position, then, Fish continues to deny that it is sharing a language and "knowing the meanings of individual words and the rules for combining them" that is involved in communication but, instead, a "way of thinking, a form of life" (p. 303). But this direct denial that the shared rules of language makes communication possible is surely bizarre, and the distinction he makes here is certainly untenable. Oddly enough, Fish's language here recalls Wittgenstein's, but in using it Wittgenstein was pointing out precisely

fact of our sharing common assumptions and ways of interpreting our common language that it would make communication impossible—we could only sit in our private worlds. But we do not; the moment we look at a piece of language and have any response whatever to its meaning, we have recognized that it is in, say, English rather than Turkish. And in so doing we are immediately sharing a convention with others, agreeing with them to use the publicly available values for linguistic structures that constitute the English language. Thus, reader-response criticism must destroy its own logical basis as soon as it tries to emerge from complete solipsism. If it tries to see *any* meaning in a text, it will have had to concede that meaning is constrained and not infinitely variable; but if it tries to argue that there are no constraints, it will be forced to abandon meaning—*all* meaning, not just fixed meaning but infinitely variable meaning, too.

Subjectivity and Objectivity   The most important root cause of this view of interpretation lies in a primitive conception of the issue of subjectivity and objectivity. The thought processes involved show the same kind of leap from one extreme to the other that we have seen before: the positions considered are limited to objectivity, on the one hand, and subjectivity, on the other. The choice is limited to these two, so that the absurdity of one extreme predisposes the choice of the other, though that, too, is no more promising. The seriously discussable positions all lie within the territory between these extremes and are ignored.

As we have already seen in the previous chapter, this kind of argument ignores the wider context of the debate over certainty and objectivity in knowledge, for in that wider context the possibility of complete certainty and objectivity was long ago abandoned. To repeat the point, the most widely held view is that all knowledge is in the nature of an hypothesis, always waiting to be overturned or modified by later insight.

---

that a language with its rules, conventions, and agreements *is* a way of thinking and form of life!

There is no piece of knowledge such that its complete objectivity can be the occasion of an inner conviction in the mind of the knower that he could not possibly be mistaken. The judgment of the community of scholars as to which of several competing views is currently the most plausible is the test of any hypothesis, and that judgment is always provisional. Knowledge, then, is neither completely objective, if by that is meant "incontrovertibly true," nor is it a matter of individually arbitrary responses that are not answerable to anything but the individual's current frame of mind. Yet all the justifications for textuality and a reader-oriented view of interpretation move from the first extreme to the second, as if abandoning the first left no possibility but the second.

This logic is clearly the basis of Tompkins's argument, which she also attributes to Culler and Fish. Objectivity is essentially the claim to know the truth; that is clearly impossible; therefore, subjectivity and the individual subjective responses of readers is the only alternative.[7] Similar logic is also the basis of Fish's curious argument that if there are two opposing views of the text, one cannot appeal to the text, because that is simply the locus of the dispute. Given Fish's logic, no knowledge of any kind is possible, for if two people make opposing statements about *anything*, the mere fact that they are different prevents any further investigation into the adequacy of either by looking at what it was that the two purported to be talking about. Once two different statements are made, according to Fish, the bare fact that they can be made not only guarantees them the equal status of being simply possible statements but also makes the matter undiscussable. The object of the discussion may not be appealed to, and no other kind of appeal is possible. Fish's assertion is rendered more plausible to him by the heavy finality of the phrase "deciding between them" when he argues that neither the text nor any-

---

[7] For more on the way theorists of criticism have traditionally set up unreal parallels between science and criticism, using absurd assumptions about the absolute objectivity of science in order to justify a laissez-faire position in criticism, see chapter six of my *The Theory of Literary Criticism: A Logical Analysis* (Berkeley, 1974).

thing else can be the "basis for deciding between them." "Deciding" obviously means here something like "establish the truth of the matter." Any lesser notion, e.g., differentiating between them, examining the evidence for one and the evidence for the other, would expose the weakness of his argument, for the text could serve as a basis for *that* and prevent the leap to our being left with only a helpless subjectivity. Ultimately, Fish's appeal to a difference of judgment between two persons comes down to this: if a point is not so obvious that *any* two persons can agree, then it is impossible to choose between two conflicting opinions and assign them different weight. Unless there is total unanimity, every opinion is equally valid.[8] And this is plainly untrue, as we must all know if we are to function at all in our everyday lives.

The subjectivity of reader-response criticism, then, is only reached via the springboard of an absolute objectivity long since abandoned in other fields of knowledge; without that outdated idea as its only alternative, there is nothing to justify a solipsistic conclusion that would make all knowledge impossible.

"One" Meaning As Opposed to Many Meanings   Another of the ways in which the theorists we are discussing reach the

---

[8] Jonathan Culler tries to reverse this issue by claiming that deconstruction, far from embodying this leap from one end of the spectrum to another, corrects traditional beliefs in showing us that it is not necessary. Having referred to the fact that mathematicians have learned to live with uncertainty, he then goes on to say, "The humanities, however, often seem troubled with the belief that a theory which asserts the ultimate indeterminacy of meaning makes all effort pointless" (*On Deconstruction*, Ithaca, 1982, p. 133). Thus, deconstructionists would be just like enlightened scientists who have understood that there are no absolutes in knowledge. But this is only one more attempt by Culler to make deconstruction sound much more reasonable than it really is. For it is surely highly doubtful whether any scientists can be found who will agree that their own adjustment to the notion that all knowledge is hypothetical (while striving for and achieving a considerable degree of precision in their results) has anything logically in common with the deconstructive advocacy of the play of signs or the resulting notion of infinite, indeterminate meaning. Contrary to Culler's unconvincing defense here, then, deconstruction does not liberate us from the conventional opposition of fixity versus freedom of meaning but, on the contrary, fully shares in it and exploits it.

position that "a poem really means whatever any reader seriously believes it to mean" or that "there is no limit to these meanings since the mind finds in the text whatever it is looking for" is through the *numerical* terminology of many, unlimited meanings, as opposed to *one* meaning.[9] To say that a text has one meaning sounds inherently very restrictive; that makes the leap to "no limit on meanings"—the typical leap to an opposite extreme—more plausible. To the extent that, in this argument, "one" meaning is the absolute certainty and objectivity of an imagined scientific method—but one that does not exist in science either—the preceding argument applies once more. But the question of singular and plural in discussing meaning requires further comment of its own.

Hamlet is a large and complex edifice of words—many thousands of them, having therefore many thousands of elements of meaning, to say nothing of the additional meaning created by their interrelations. To say that *Hamlet* has *one* meaning is to say something strange, regardless of the particular theory of meaning being employed.[10] It is, surely, a complex of meanings. There is one sense only in which a singular could be used: *Hamlet* is a unique text, not like any other. There is only one *Hamlet* in this sense; but in any other kind of context, the singular is not very appropriate. If, then, one wishes to use a plural in connection with the meanings in the text of *Hamlet*, that is well and good: there are many words, many lines, many characters. But if the plural in this context is used to throw doubt on the singularity and uniqueness of *Hamlet*, as opposed to *Macbeth*, we have confused two different usages and contexts. Criticism, if it is to do anything of value, must approach *Hamlet* as a text that is distinctive and

---

[9] There is some irony in Steven Rendall's using an argument by Montaigne, to the effect that a text has an infinite number of meanings, to serve as a vehicle for his own advocacy of this position, for in so doing he is attributing this, rather than that, meaning to Montaigne, i.e., a position distinctively different from other possible positions. If Montaigne can mean anything, like all other texts, how can he specifically mean what Rendall says he means?

[10] Cf. Graff, "Deconstruction as Dogma," *Georgia Review* 34 (1980), p. 421: "the concept of a 'single' interpretation could not legitimately be maintained by anyone since it is nonsensical."

unlike *Macbeth*: if *Hamlet* can mean an *infinite* range of meanings and can be whatever the mind takes it to be, it can presumably mean whatever *Macbeth* means. *Hamlet* is one thing; *Macbeth* is another; but this "one" is not the one of the context of *Hamlet* meaning only one thing. The mathematical terms *one*, *many*, and *infinite* only serve to confuse the issues.

The common term for multiple rather than single meaning is of course *ambiguity*, but it presents further possibilities for misconceptions. Literary texts are often ambiguous, of course—but *any* piece of language can be ambiguous in the same sense. Widening the frame of reference of our discussion to other fields once more makes it easy to see the error of deconstructive arguments. Nothing seems more precise than the language of geometry, but there, as anywhere, we cannot escape the ambiguity that results from the limit of the specificity of a particular term. A quadrangle is a four-sided figure. A rectangle is a four-sided right-angled figure. A rhombus is a four-sided non-right-angled figure. The word *quadrangle* can thus refer to both. Does this mean that the word is ambiguous? Yes and no; like most words, it has a certain level of specificity, which makes its intended meaning quite clear but which will also leave us with the judgment that it is ambiguous *in contexts where we have an interest in greater specificity*. If we were interested in the distinction rhombus/rectangle, the word *quadrangle* will seem ambiguous. But that has nothing whatsoever to do with any uncertainty as to the meaning of the word; while lamenting its ambiguity *in context*, we know perfectly well what quadrangle means. Questions of ambiguity in literary texts likewise usually concern level of specificity, not lack of determinate meaning. What does *Macbeth* mean when Macbeth says to Banquo, "fail not our feast," and Banquo replies, "My lord, I will not"? Does it mean that Banquo will come back to haunt Macbeth (as he does)? Or just that Banquo, when saying it, expresses his *intent* to come, his state of mind at that moment, and nothing more? Literary critics used to worry about choosing one or the other until the New Critics started to realize that ambiguity could on occasion have positive value and concluded that it can easily have *both* meanings. But if that sounded startling, it was really not. All that the New Critics were really saying was that the level of specificity of this language is not such as to require a choice, and (such is language) if nothing in the context *requires* the choice to be made, it cannot be made and is not made. A quadrangle remains a quadrangle unless something in the context makes it more specifically a rectangle; a tree remains a tree until something in the context specifies it as an oak. It would make no sense to harp on the "infinite" meanings of "tree" where no species is specified; the word clearly has some constraints that limit it to far less than infinity (it is *not* a flower) but it has no constraint as to species. None of this has anything to do with a text having two unrelated meanings or no clear meaning at all or meaning whatever the reader wants it to mean; on the contrary, if one treats the lines in question from *Macbeth* in deconstructive terms, one cannot even recognize the operation of that ambiguity that is their most distinctive feature. For it is precisely the fact that *two* specific meanings play against each other that is the point of these lines. To say that these lines have an infinity of meanings would be to miss this particular, highly significant ambiguity by submerging it beneath an indiscriminate, shapeless chaos of meanings. The important conclusion here, then, is that even ambiguity requires *specificity* for it to work; textuality would destroy it, too, along with all other meaning in a text, by making that text too indeterminate even for ambiguity to be visible.

This point, however, reminds us of the inconsistency between the two major critical strands in deconstruction. The strand discussed in chapter three dealt with specific meanings, two being emphasized—the surface and its opposite; but the one that I have discussed in this chapter makes *all* meanings equally relevant. These are two quite different positions—the one cannot coexist with the other. Neither will stand up to scrutiny, but there is no doubt that the second is the more incoherent of the two. The first deals, however rigidly and incautiously, with specific things that a text can mean; but if, following the second, texts can mean anything, then they really mean nothing.

The Development of Knowledge through Conflicting Assertions   Textuality and reader-oriented interpretation focus on the opinions of particular readers in a curiously static way. When Fish tells us that if two readers disagree there is no way of appealing to the text to decide the issue between them, he leaves us with two people and two opinions that never come into contact with each other; they remain what they are, never meet, and therefore never modify. But this is an unreal supposition: in the real world in which we live, progress in all fields occurs through the clash of different views and of conflicting opinions. In that clash, views do not simply persevere unaltered; the world does *not* consist of individuals stubbornly clinging to their first thoughts and not talking to others. On the contrary, individuals present their views for discussion by others, and there is modification, alteration, even abandonment of ideas in the process of discussion. Some views are persuasive and grow in influence; others do not persuade and are forgotten. The development of knowledge is a *social* process: argument between differing individuals counts for a great deal in this process, and appeal to the text under discussion is, contrary to Fish's view, an important part of that argument. In the world of Fish's example, critic X forms his view, sticks to it, refuses to take part in any analysis or evaluation of it, and simply insists that, because it is his view, regardless of whether he can support it or persuade anyone to it, it must be allowed to stand as one possibility among others, with all equal. The real situation is quite different. If critic X produces a view that cannot persuade anybody but himself over a long period, his view does not survive; the arena of viewpoints that are still seriously discussable will no longer have a place for it. This is as true in criticism as it is in the sciences. If one individual maintains that the earth is flat, we are not compelled to say that that fact alone makes his view equal to any other. Nor need we say, with Fish, that no appeal to the object under discussion is possible, because that is the source of the disagreement; and still less need we be intimidated by the bugaboo of total objectivity into failing to distinguish between different degrees of plausibility. Argument, back and forth, moves knowledge and opinion forward; reader-response criticism seems so intent on protecting the individual's right to any opinion he or she wishes to have that it makes everyone a windowless monad that cannot communicate with any other. In so doing, it shuts its eyes to how inquiry actually proceeds—through the clash of differing viewpoints and the consequent winnowing out of those that cannot hold up.

So MUCH for the flaws in the argument for textuality and for the sanctity of the individual reader's response, whatever its character. But how, it may be asked, could so unpromising an argument have achieved any currency? The answer to this is that this view of criticism speaks to an emotional attitude that has long been widespread among critics. In this sense, deconstruction and reader-response theory are not new but reflect and reformulate critical prejudices that had been around for a very long time. To this point I shall return more generally in my last chapter, in assessing the causes and significance of deconstruction in the contemporary critical scene; for the moment, it suffices to say that textuality is only a radical formulation of the traditional laissez-faire attitude of that strain of literary criticism that has always wanted above all else to be free to do and say whatever it wished, without being held accountable or required to justify it. Laissez-faire criticism, too, has always supported itself with an unreal view of science as a realm of absolute certainties, the point of which was to allow the critic to act as if he or she were not subject to control by evidence or by judgments of cogency. Here deconstruction, far from breaking new ground, retreats into old attitudes. Even the view that the critic is like the artist, and on a par with the artist, is nothing new; it, too, was a frequently observed part of the old complex of attitudes.[11] There is, then, nothing

---

[11] See my *The Theory of Literary Criticism*, chapters three and six, for further discussion of these attitudes.

shocking or revolutionary about these tendencies. On the other hand, there is no doubt that deconstruction has had an effect on the current critical scene; these unproductive attitudes in criticism have been strengthened and emboldened. A few examples will illustrate that effect.

Literary texts claim our attention as texts of unique character: whatever we think *Hamlet* means, its special character is not like that of any other text. Criticism's task is to address this specific quality of *Hamlet*. Are we, in actual practice, really willing to give up that aim and let the critic find whatever he wants to in a text? Adopting a theory means living with its consequences; but let us look at those consequences in two particular situations that are fairly typical of what has occurred recently. The situations are taken from my own special field in criticism—criticism of German literature—but essentially similar ones are being seen with increasing frequency in criticism generally.

In the first of the situations, a scholar writes a book on E.T.A. Hoffmann, the thesis of which is that the key to his work is its obsession with sexual guilt and unacknowledged sexual shame. For the moment, let us not consider whether this seems appropriate to such works as *The Golden Pot, The Devil's Elixirs, The Sandman*, and so on; what is relevant to this story is that the same author also writes a book about Heinrich von Kleist, the thesis of which is that Kleist's work, too, is all about sexual guilt and unacknowledged sexual shame. The complete repetition will certainly surprise readers who have always been able to recognize strong, distinctive differences between Kleist and Hoffmann, and it will probably puzzle all those familiar with Kleist's greatest works, *Michael Kohlhaas* and the *Prinz von Homburg*. But the same author also writes a study of Kafka, and here it turns out that Kafka, too, is all about sexual guilt and unacknowledged sexual shame.[12] By now, a judgment of this situation will be irresist-

---

[12] These are all works by James McGlathery: *Mysticism and Sexuality: E.T.A. Hoffmann* (Las Vegas, Berne, Frankfort/Main, 1981); *Desire's Sway: The Plays and Stories of Heinrich von Kleist* (Detroit, 1983); "Desire's Per-

ible: this recurrent idea has its source in the mind of the scholar concerned, not in the work of Hoffmann, Kleist, and Kafka. That there is some overlap in the thematic concerns of different authors is not difficult to believe; but that a variety of very different writers really all have the same predominant concern is another matter. Surely, no one should pay much attention to criticism when it is, as here, clear that the ideas presented have little to do with the writers who are the *claimed* subject of the criticism. But let us imagine that we are committed to the theory of criticism that we have been discussing: what can textuality and reader-response criticism do for us here? Fish can only tell us that it is no use appealing to the characteristics of the texts, because they are the locus of the disagreement between us and this particular critic. And so, no matter how obvious it is that Hoffmann is not Kleist and Kleist not Kafka, if only one critic says that he perceives them to be essentially the same, not only must we take this claim seriously, but the very fact that it is made prevents us from disputing it: we cannot appeal to the fact that the texts look most unalike because, according to Fish, if there are conflicting views of the text, the text as the locus of the conflict cannot settle that conflict. Tompkins, on the other hand, would only be able to tell us that to think we see differences between Kafka, Hoffman, and Kleist is to fall victim to the myth of absolute objectivity and to claim to know an absolute truth. Rendall's view will be that there is no limit to what the mind can see in Kafka, Kleist, and Hoffman—and logically that will have to include the fact that the mind can see the very same things in all these if it wants to. Donato will insist that words only refer to other words and that there is nothing really there to interpret anyway. If, then, we have the sense that some interpretations seem utterly silly, while others do not, that is an illusion. Crosman can only tell us that a text means whatever a reader seriously wants it to mean: if the mind wants Kleist to mean the same thing as Kafka, so be it. None of these

___
secutions in Kafka's 'Judgement,' 'Metamorphosis,' and 'A Country Doctor,' " *Perspectives in Contemporary Literature* 7 (1981), pp. 54–63.

theorists will allow us to discriminate, to choose between what looks at least worth taking seriously and what seems immediately dismissible.

Before drawing any conclusion from the helplessness of this kind of critical standpoint when faced with my first example, let me turn to the second. I recently received an essay to referee for a journal in the field of German literature. The essay simply expounded three different interpretations, taken from published criticism, of a story by Kleist—interpretations that were clearly mutually exclusive—and concluded that this was a good example of the deconstructive thesis that literary texts were capable, because of the free play of signs, of an infinite variety of interpretations. Given this framework, there is no room for a kind of discrimination that seems essential from a practical standpoint: it is impossible in principle to decide whether one or the other of the three might be more or less enlightening or that one or the other might be fanciful or even irrelevant to the text's actual words and composition. In fact, the article in question did not approach in any way the matter of how the text might relate to any of the interpretations. It was simply sufficient, in the mind of the author of the study, to accept that these three interpretations existed. Scrutiny of them, analysis of their cogency, judgment of their strength— all of this is not simply ignored by accident—it is ignored *in principle*. I spoke above of a *practical* need in such situations. Such is the volume of printed material that no one could hope to read a small fraction of all that is published. We are compelled to make choices to read this rather than that; how are we to decide to read and take seriously this rather than that volume of criticism? The essay to which I refer rules out the choice from the outset. Now the inability to monitor the *quality* of criticism is a serious omission, but textuality is committed to this omission as a matter of principle. For Rendall, choosing between differing interpretations on the basis of relative degrees of appropriateness to the literary text would involve the false humility of the critic's being subservient to the text. For Donato, since criticism is also literature, it involves an act of creation not subject to any controls. For Fish, we cannot appeal to the text to see which interpretation works better, because that would ignore the fact that the text produced the differing interpretations. For Tompkins, any limitation on the critic smacks of a belief in objectivity. And for Crosman, discrimination among interpretations would reduce the infinite number of possible meanings of a literary text.

We have reached one of those points in theory where it is necessary to face squarely what it is that a particular theory commits us to; and this one commits us to two end results that are amazing. First, we are unable to *discriminate* when faced with a number of differing interpretations; second, it must be quite unnecessary to offer argument or support for one's interpretation and a waste of time to do so. The second must follow from the first: argument and evidence in support of an interpretation are only needed if we are trying to judge whether that interpretation is better or worse supported than any other interpretation—but if we are committed to the view that an infinite variety of interpretations can exist and that no priority can be established among them, then argument for one or the other becomes irrelevant.

When a theory has such embarrassing consequences as these, any prudent theorist will surely have the courage to admit that the theory went badly wrong somewhere and must be abandoned. No position that relies on this complete dismissal of argument and support for a viewpoint can be taken seriously. What is completely lost from view when all responses to a text stand unexamined, is that we do *not* simply get a response from a critic; we get his or her reasoning and explanation, too. The critic is expected to, and always does, explain the reasons for his view. He argues the *case for* his interpretation. Reading a critic is not just a process of receiving his conclusions—it involves looking at his argument and forming a judgment of its cogency. None of this has anything to do with a belief in objective truth. In any field of inquiry, ideas are advanced and argued for, and the arguments are weighed against those of competing positions.

Textuality's infinity of meanings in a text is, in practice, a pernicious doctrine: it encourages us to stop discriminating, to stop *thinking* about interpretations and their strengths and weaknesses. For to tell us that competing conceptions of a text are simply part of the limitless creativity of the reader in confronting the text is to tell us not to evaluate any of them and neither to discard even the most fanciful nor to prefer the most cogent: they simply exist, and that is that. But this attitude to criticism misunderstands the function of imagination and creativity just as much as it ignores the function of argument. Imagination and creativity are vital aspects of all thought, in science just as in philosophy and criticism. Deconstruction is not wrong to say that the critic is creative; where it is disastrously wrong, however, is in its assumption that creativity means freedom from constraints or from standards of judgment operating on it results. Creativity is not simply achieved by letting the mind wander with complete freedom into thoughts never previously recorded; in any sphere of activity, we judge someone to have been creative only if he produces an idea that is *both* original *and* valuable. A new idea in a business concern that results in a highly successful new venture is called creative; one that results in bankruptcy is called a piece of folly. Creativity is surely needed in criticism and is to be valued there—but that cannot mean that the critic is free to say what he will and that we cannot evaluate whether what he has said makes any sense. To be creative is not to let one's imagination run free: it is to use the imagination *productively*. The very notion of creativity is degraded when it is thought of as operating randomly, without being responsive to the entire situation in which it operates.

The basic stance of this view of criticism, then, must be damaging to the quality of criticism. If creativity operates without constraint, there is no need to think and *rethink* one's train of thought; no need to hesitate and ponder whether the results really do seem appropriate to Shakespeare or Kleist or Hoffmann; no need to judge whether one's ideas are persuasive or compelling; no need to worry about whether Kafka can in any meaningful way be seen as thematically identical to Kleist. What the critic has done, he has done; let no one question it, let no one analyze and evaluate it, and let no one have second thoughts about it either. In practice, many critics who advocate textuality do not really accept its consequences, but this critical stance has nonetheless had enough influence on the practice of criticism to cause a measurable decline in its quality. Criticism used to be thought of as the art of discrimination—discriminating between the unique quality of one great writer and that of another or between talented, careful writing and writing that lacks quality. But it must follow from deconstruction and reader-response theory that we can neither discriminate between the qualities of great writers nor between great and poor writers nor between good and poor criticism; and so an intellectual laziness is encouraged. We produce our own thoughts and words but need not concern ourselves whether they might be improved upon, by ourselves or others. Perhaps the strangest aspect of this situation is that this view of criticism is advocated as a more sophisticated and complex position, the operations of "normal" criticism being looked down on as simpler and more primitive. But these judgments obviously need reversing; nothing is simpler and more primitive than insisting on one's own individual response, while real discrimination requires the critic to go well beyond that initial stage of thought. Complexity and sophistication will demand more thought and analysis and more careful discrimination between the characteristics of differing texts, not less.

Shakespeare's texts are the result of many individual decisions on his part to write this, rather than that.[13] Is it really "false modesty" for the critic to think that he should pay close attention to those decisions and the emphases that result from them? Shakespeare's critic cannot fail to be impressed by the fact that thousands of critics write on him each year and that

[13] This point has, of course, nothing to do with the issues present in the controversy over the intentional fallacy and thus nothing to do with the author's control or lack of control over the meaning of his own text. The author's understanding of what he has done in setting a particular shape for a text is one thing, and it may be judged more or less adequate. That he *did* choose a particular form of words is a separate question, one not involving issues of the author's possibly incomplete understanding of his own action.

his plays are performed in hundreds of theaters. These facts and others like them explain what it means to say that Shakespeare is considered the greatest writer in the English language. It is hardly false modesty for the critic, faced with this awesome record, to assume that he is not Shakespeare's equal in creativity and that the products of Shakespeare's mind, not those of his own, are the focus of interest in his criticism. Once again, the consequences of deconstruction's textuality must be allowed to reflect on its logic, and these are truly absurd consequences. Surely these consequences should have impelled advocates of reader-response criticism and textuality to go back and think again about the logical steps that led them to their theory. It is to a more general examination of this kind of logic that I now turn.

CHAPTER SIX

The Logic of Deconstruction

IN PREVIOUS CHAPTERS I have analyzed a number of particular issues in deconstructive thought, but deconstruction is not just a collection of arguments in different areas of theory or even a group of related doctrines; it is possible to abstract from all of this a particular strategy, a kind of deconstructive logic of inquiry or, as advocates themselves put it, a *performance* of a distinctive kind. This typical performance deserves close attention. By generalizing from the particular deconstructive arguments we have analyzed, we shall see more clearly what the deconstructive performance is and be in a position to focus both on the strength of its appeal and on the nature of its underlying logic.

The moves made in the typical deconstructive performance are sufficiently regular that they can be schematized. In the first step, the argument fixes on one of a small number of traditional central problems in literary theory. These problems usually represent particular versions of broader problems in thought and inquiry in general: the fundamental issue of the relation of words to things; the issue of certainty in knowledge (are there any absolute truths?), the issue of the meaning of a literary text (does the text have any stable meaning independent of a reader's experience?), the issue of interpretations of literary texts (can they be justified, or are they merely individual?), the issue of the intention of a speaker or author (does the author's perspective control the meaning of a text, and must it simply mean what its author intended?)

Deconstruction begins by focusing on the naive, common-sense viewpoint on each particular issue in order to undermine it, or to "put it in question" and to "problematise" it. By contrast, the beginning of other attempts to advance thought is normally taken to require a focus on the highest and most advanced level of thinking that has been achieved on a given question; we start with the latest state of the art and try to go on from there. Deconstructionist thinking shifts the context we begin with, away from the most sophisticated thought achieved to date, on to unsophisticated, simple notions.[1] This involves considerable loss. When dealing with meaning, for example, the deconstructive approach is to focus immediately upon the simple belief that words refer directly to things; deconstructionists develop their argument by stressing the naiveté of that view, in so doing avoiding the advanced, subtle work of many decades that has made this view hardly worth bothering with any more in any reasonably sophisticated context. Or when discussing the issue of certainty in knowledge, deconstruction tends to begin with the naive belief in clear, certain knowledge rather than the work in philosophy of science that abandoned that idea long ago. In the matter of the meaning in literary texts, the view made the center of attention in the deconstructive argument is that literary texts have a clear and statable meaning, which again ignores the fact that in the endless discussions of objectivity and subjectivity in criticism, very few have ever committed themselves to such a view. The consensus of critics for some time has been that literary texts are inexhaustible. On the author's intention, the center of attention for deconstruction is the view that the author's intent determines meaning. Again, it is attacked as if still omnipresent and as if it had never been questioned before. Thus the long debate on the intentional fallacy in Anglo-American theory, in which the majority view of theorists has been that the author's intent does not control the meaning of a literary work, is ignored.

Having thus concentrated on the most naive viewpoint and

[1] The one notable exception here is Saussure, certainly a complex thinker on the theory of meaning. But it soon becomes apparent that Derrida really wants to talk about the primitive belief in immediate "presence" of meaning and that he wants to diagnose that belief in Saussure. Saussure is a curious example to pick—it is much harder to see this belief in his writings than would have been the case for many others. But, as I have argued in chapter two, this is surely a misreading of Saussure; and so Derrida chooses as a representative of this viewpoint a thinker who brilliantly demolished it.

made it the datum from which the argument must begin and having generally avoided scholarship that had already taken these issues to a far higher level of complexity, the deconstructive argument moves to its next stage, which supplies a polar opposite to be set beside the naive beliefs with which the argument began. For example, words do not refer to things in the real world but only signify other words; authors do not create the meaning of their texts by composing them, but instead readers, by reading them; texts do not have a particular meaning that can be investigated but are limitless in their meaning because of the free play of signs; a careful reading does not give knowledge of a text, because all readings are misreadings; whatever the obvious meaning of a literary text is taken to be, one must stand that meaning on its head.

From this point on, there is some inconsistency. Much of the time, the logic of "neither/nor and either/or" predominates; the simple view is not rejected but "displaced," and the opposition of the two extremes is retained and deconstructed. But it is also fair to say that this theoretical quasi-neutrality often seems to break down, in Derrida's case as well as in his followers, and to result in a strong tilt toward the polar opposite of the naive belief from which the argument begins. The exposition of the alternative pole of free play is so unrestrained and enthusiastic that Derrida's followers can surely take this, without distorting his text, to amount to advocacy of it; the contemptuous labeling of its opposite as ethnocentric, or simple-minded, can easily be read as rejection, and in practice it is taken to be so by Derrida's readers. In sum, the contrast of the warm, lengthy, seemingly unreserved elaboration of the one with the denunciation of the other does not seem to add up to a "neither/nor, either/or"—but instead to a "not this, but that." In like fashion, the author's intent is presented as a notion that restricts while textuality liberates, and accordingly the enthusiastic embracing of the latter contrasts markedly with the denunciation of the shortcomings of the former. The emotional weight of deconstructionist writings leans heavily to positions that reverse and stand on their head the naive beliefs from which the argument begins, regardless of the claims for a "neither/nor and either/or" logic. From our point of view, however, it scarcely matters whether one takes the position of those deconstructionists who insist that that logic is always controlling, and never forgotten, or those who simply embrace and advocate ideas such as free play and textuality; the logical objections to either one of these two positions are much the same, and they are decisive. Primitive ideas reversed produce more primitive ideas; the jump from one extreme to another is not productive thinking whether one takes the second to have *replaced* the first or *displaced* it. Free play is an incoherent notion whether one takes it by itself or as a package together with the equally incoherent notion that was there before it. Or, as we saw in chapter one, Mallarmé's being simply a Platonist or simply not a Platonist are equally crude and uninteresting ideas, and to say that they are both and neither true and false adds nothing of substance to them—they are still uninteresting ideas.

A further typical feature of deconstructionist arguments can be seen in its manner of introducing the idea that is the polar opposite of the initial naive belief. This is essentially and inevitably dramatic and gives the production of the reversal a provocative quality, one of iconoclasm. Accordingly, there is heavy emphasis on moral terminology in deconstructive writings. Deconstruction is "disturbing," "disruptive," it "unmasks," "subverts," "dismantles," "exposes," "challenges," and, a favorite word, it is a "scandal."[2] But with these emo-

---

[2] Often these moralistic terms seem strangely out of place in an intellectual context. Take, for example, Geoffrey Hartman's allusion to the "scandal of figurative language" (*Criticism in the Wilderness*, Yale, 1980, p. 31). We are all familiar with the use of the word *scandal* from contexts such as Watergate. Has figurative language or a viewpoint on figurative language ever produced a situation in which tongues wagged as in a genuine scandal? Do issues of metaphorical language really command that kind of attention? The word *scandal* suggests extreme boldness of action and an affront to the small-minded; its use in intellectual contexts is therefore more than a little self-congratulatory. The use of this word in deconstruction has its origin in Derrida himself, however; e.g., "Structure, Sign, and Play in the Discourse of the Human Sciences" in *The Structuralist Controversy*, ed. Richard Macksey and Eugenio Donato (Baltimore and London, 1972), p. 260: "One could say—

tional gains come considerable intellectual losses. If an idea is to make a dramatic impact, it needs to be simple and direct, and so this is one more factor that tends towards a primitive kind of notion as the counter to the initial commonsense starting point. There is no room in this process for the gain in intellectual complexity that comes from looking carefully at the formulation of the commonsense notion, and the way in which it poses the question, in order to leave it behind not by reversal but by discarding its terms completely. And once more, this rush from one end of the spectrum to the other inevitably leaps over and avoids previous thought on these issues, thought that had frequently explored what lies between the two ends of the spectrum with considerable subtlety. For example, Wimsatt and Beardsley on intention, Wittgenstein and J. R. Firth on how verbal categories relate to the world of things, Dilthey on the logic of humanistic inquiry, C. S. Peirce on knowledge and hypothesis—all of these and many others like them are ignored in this process of beginning with primitive theoretical ideas and the dramatic leap to their opposite pole (and back, as the case may be). A reversal of the terms of a simple-minded position will produce only an equally simple-minded position; it changes direction without increasing complexity.

How, then, does so unproductive a procedure manage to maintain a semblance of being exciting and complex nonetheless? Two factors seem to me important. I have already pointed to the emotional component in the performance. By keeping attention fixed on the initial simple view that is to be displaced and making the denunciation of that view a central aspect of the whole performance (rather than merely a starting point that is to be left behind and forgotten), deconstruction creates a sense of the excitement of intellectual progress beyond the commonplace, of the drama of intellectual confrontation, and of the exhilaration of provocativeness. Formula-

---

rigorously using that word whose scandalous signification is always obliterated in French—that this movement of the foreplay, permitted by the lack, the absence of a center or origin, is the movement of *supplementarity*."

tions are chosen not for their logical or intellectual appropriateness but, instead, for their drama and shock. Extremes of formulation are thus *required*; they are not simply the product of intellectual inadequacy but an essential and required part of deconstruction.

But there is a second and even more important means that deconstruction employs to maintain a semblance of viability: the issues are generally cast in new and strange terminology so that familiar positions may not seem so familiar and otherwise obviously relevant scholarship may not seem so obviously relevant. The attack on the reference theory of meaning is translated into an attack on the "metaphysics of presence," though both are essentially the same rather naive view of the relation of words and things; but the new terms make the issue seem different and help to conceal the otherwise embarrassing fact that Derrida, in mounting this attack, does not come to terms with the large body of writing that has already performed this task. To reject the reference theory might seem too obviously commonplace; to attack "the metaphysics of presence" is to attack at least a new set of words, if not ideas.

Extraordinary verbal complexity is not excluded by this concern with primitive ideas; no one could deny that Derrida's texts are extraordinarily difficult and obscure. But though, for example, his making Husserl the starting point for a discussion of meaning in *La Voix et le Phénomène* involves him immediately in highly convoluted and difficult writing, it is Husserl's simple and logically vulnerable assumptions about intentions, reference, and essences (i.e., that speech is the vehicle for conveying meaning and intention that is separate from itself) that draw him to begin there. Simple ideas are not incompatible with tortuous prose—on the contrary, it is when the clouds of tortuous prose are dispelled that primitive ideas are often found hiding from a light that they could not survive.

The English-speaking deconstructionist has an additional resource here, in that he can use derivatives of Derrida's original French text, which adds another layer of strangeness to his terminology. For example, it might not seem too radical for anyone to suggest that entrenched orthodoxy in any field of inquiry needs to be scrutinized carefully and that we should always be on our guard in order not to be obstructed by moribund ideas like, for example, the reference theory of language. But this rather familiar injunction is given new lustre as we are told that we must "demystify privileged ideas." And if one wishes to enter the debate over the author's intention in criticism without being seen to repeat familiar arguments, one can add the deconstructive air of drama and avoid the dull, academic phraseology of Wimsatt and Beardsley (e.g., the intention of the author is neither available nor usable as an exclusive standard for judging or interpreting the literary work) by announcing "the death of the author." In like manner, the familiar and long-standing critical resistance to any final interpretation of a text is given a new air with the more dramatic "all interpretation is misinterpretation." (Who would listen if it were merely said that no one view of a text can be considered the final word on it?)

Another example is found in the deconstructive vocabulary for the bias of individual critics. A familiar version of this is the idea that a critic's individual temperament, ideology, and outlook will color his or her view of a text and that none of us can escape from this fact. Deconstruction needs to make much of this familiar point and to make it in such a way that it will seem a *deconstructive* point, not available elsewhere. The solution is to talk not of critical bias or individual temperament but, instead, of "desire," "blindness," "fatigue"; all words that are not previously found in this context, to be sure, but their very strangeness (and mild inappropriateness, therefore) to the context makes them seem to do something new.[3] But they do not: they simply restate the familiar issue.

My last example concerns the word *deconstruction* itself, for the familiar pattern can be seen in its arrival, too. The first step is to focus on the most literal, surface meaning of a text, avoiding any attention to subtleties it may contain. The next step is to demonstrate that there is a second layer of meaning,

[3] Barbara Johnson, "Nothing Fails Like Success," *SCE Reports* 8 (Fall 1980), p. 14.

an ironic layer, or one indicated in imagery and metaphor rather than in the literal meaning. And in the final step the familiarity of this procedure—it has, after all, been part of the stock-in-trade of critics for a very long time—is disguised by exotic new terminology: what we have done is not simply to look carefully at the different layers of textual meaning—we have "deconstructed" it, "demythologized" it. And, to reinforce the exotic terminology, any discrepancy between the levels of textual meaning is stated in a highly dramatic, provocative fashion; that different levels have frequently been found to be discrepant is, again, too familiar in previous criticism to leave it unadorned.

These, then, are the essentials of the deconstructive logic: a logic not well adapted to productive, original thinking, but rather to creating its illusion. This analysis is both confirmed by and explains the sometimes baffling behavior of deconstructionists when they are under attack. Anyone who has engaged in an exchange on deconstruction will have noticed that the defense takes very standard forms. The defensive moves correspond exactly to the essentials of deconstructive logic. An objection is met first of all by attributing to the objector the simple, naive view that is the starting point for the issues under discussion. Sometimes the attribution is reasonable enough, as it was in the case of M. H. Abrams's claim for critical objectivity and certainty. But in most cases the objector is left wondering how and why such a view could be abstracted from what he has said. The rejection of the objection corresponds in its tone to the impassioned, dramatic denunciation seen in the second step of deconstructive logic: objectors to deconstruction are never handled gently, for they must always take the role of the naive believer who must be denounced. The only terms available for the dispute, from the deconstructionist's point of view, are the contrast of traditionalist naiveté, on the one hand, and the sophistication of its deconstructionist debunkers, on the other. The possibility of a radically different kind of debate—say, that between two different kinds of revisionists of traditional views—is not recognized. It is not recognized because deconstruction depends on its not existing.

But the third rule of deconstructionist defense is perhaps the most noteworthy, perhaps because it is on occasion (though very rarely) breached, with interesting results. That rule is never consent to a change of terminology and always insist that the wording of the deconstructive argument is sacrosanct. The reason for this is obvious enough. To say that the prevailing view of a literary text has missed an ironic level of its meaning sounds very familiar from countless critical books and articles over many decades; to say that one should demystify privileged readings of texts sounds newer, more important, more *theoretical* and modern. If the deconstructionist consents to the change to the more familiar formulation, his uniquely and distinctively deconstructive position has suddenly evaporated.

Lest I be misunderstood here, I should make more clear what I am saying and what I am *not* saying. I am not saying that the precise, actual terms of an argument are not important; plainly, they are. But it is one thing to make the *general* point that two different sets of terms cannot always be assumed to be functionally equivalent in a given context; it is quite another thing to face the issue in the *specific* way demanded by a particular situation. To do that, it would be necessary to argue against the change of terms by showing that in this particular case the substitute terms are functionally quite different, and thus that the *substance* of the argument had been changed by the substitution. If the deconstructive defense were to be made in this way, it would be perfectly valid: one set of terms should indeed not be assumed to be interchangeable with another until it is established that whatever differences there are between the two sets are not relevant to the specific argument under consideration. But the defense is not valid if it consists only in an objection to the change of terms as inherently unfair to the deconstructionist argument *simply* because of the change and without any demonstration of the discrepancies between the two sets of terms and their effect on this particular argument. If deconstructionists want to object to the replacement of the exotic terms with more familiar ones and with this to object that their essential argument has not been faithfully preserved in the new terms but is in fact misstated by them, they must show what has been removed from the argument by showing the discrepancy between the sets of terms.

The claim that any change of terms must *ipso facto* be a distortion is therefore insufficient; but that claim would not only be false but also completely inconsistent with the rest of the deconstructionist position. As to the first of these points, two different terms cannot perform exactly *all* of the same functions in all possible contexts—otherwise they would not be different. But they can perform *some* of the same functions in some contexts, and those functions may be the ones that are dominant and most relevant to a dispute between the deconstructionist and his opponent. It is up to deconstructionists to show that the important issues in the given context will not allow the substitution and give their reasons. But as to the second point, an insistence on the inviolability of a given set of terms would constitute a most amusing abdication of the deconstructive view of meaning. For the theory of textuality and of the play of signs allows words and texts to mean and mean ad infinitum and forbids any attempt to specify meaning in precise terms; yet to insist that only the original terms of an argument will do and that their meaning cannot be conveyed by any substitution is to take a position on the meaning of a given term that is, above all, a very rigid one: the meaning of a particular word is now said to be so *specific* that it cannot be matched by any other word or string of words. Obviously, deconstruction is completely inconsistent with that position.

It is only a small step from insisting on the irreplaceability of the unfamiliar, rather exotic terms,[4] to insisting on the value and inviolability of obscurity; but the same issues are present in both cases, and the same kinds of logical objections

---

[4] Or, as George McFadden not unreasonably calls them, "magic" terms, in his review of de Man's, *Allegories of Reading*, in *Journal of Aesthetics and Art Criticism* 39 (1981), p. 341.

are decisive. The underlying need, once again, is to resist any attempt to translate the argument into terms that allow it to be related to existing scholarship, lest it become apparent that there is not very much to that argument when set in the wider context of existing thought. And here some additional factors intervene, for example, the equation of obscurity and profundity that has been readily available in European thought since Kant and Hegel and, in addition, a quasi-moral appeal: an obscure text is difficult, and difficulty presents a *challenge* to readers. To attempt to clarify, so the argument runs, is to seek safety, to fail this moral challenge.

This may achieve some superficial plausibility, but it lacks one crucial element that would be necessary to make it really convincing, and in the absence of that element, it fails. For this argument, too, can only succeed as a *particular* one, relevant to a particular situation: it cannot stand as a *general* claim. Consider what would happen if we were to accept it as a general claim: obscurity would, in effect, have become an independent value, and obscure ideas could no longer be penetrated by investigation and analysis. We should be forced to accept any idea for which its inventor claims the magical property of obscurity. Plainly, then, what is needed for this defense of obscurity in deconstruction to succeed is not a general invocation of the value of obscurity but a demonstration of its necessity in this *particular* case. If the original "difficult" and "challenging" terms contain elements that cannot be conveyed in a paraphrase, then it should be possible to contrast the paraphrase and the original in order to show what has been lost and wherein the discrepancy between the two sets of terms lies. But this kind of particular argument is never given; instead, we are given only the general argument, always by itself insufficient, that translation to more familiar terms "domesticates" and "tames" these radical new ideas. (Again, let us remember that here, too, the insistence on the unique specificity of meaning of a particular set of terms is inconsistent with an insistence on the free play of signs.)

To make the case here against deconstruction, it is not necessary to condemn obscurity or difficulty in an argument as simply a failure of exposition and a falling-off from the universal standard of clarity and simplicity. Some ideas and arguments are inherently difficult; some obscure prose is well worth the effort to grasp and understand. The point is simply that it is never possible to appeal to the difficulty of an argument to veto investigation and analysis of it. To the contrary, in the case of ideas that are obscure and difficult, efforts must be redoubled to inspect them very carefully, to analyze, to scrutinize, to reformulate in many different ways. It is extraordinary to claim that it is precisely in the case of difficult ideas that this must not be done; and in the absence of any specific argument to back up this strange claim, it will inevitably seem designed to protect from serious scrutiny an intellectual position that might not stand up to such scrutiny.

At this point it is instructive to consider again the anomalous position within deconstruction of Jonathan Culler: solidly part of the movement, surely, and prominent as the most lucid of its apologists and yet treated with suspicion and, on occasion, contempt by many within it.[5] The explanation of this paradox follows the fundamental shape of deconstructive logic. Perhaps uniquely, Culler attempts to explain deconstruction in terms that can be *understood,* in language that communicates what is to be communicated. But this disturbs precarious protective devices; once the exotic terms or provocative formulations have been penetrated, what is exposed is often too commonplace to be interesting. When, for example, Culler explains that the shocking claim "all interpretation is misinterpretation" simply means that no interpretation can ever be final, he gives the game away; what is revealed is a trivial position. If that is what "all interpretation is misinterpretation" meant, it was not worth making any fuss about. No wonder deconstructionists are ambivalent about Culler's proselytizing and attempting to reach a wider audience for them. Steven Rendall exemplifies this ambivalence with two different kinds of judgment, which are surely not consistent

<hr>

[5] See Rendall and Lentricchia, as cited in chapter one, note 5, above.

with each other.[6] On the one hand, Culler has a gift for expounding difficult ideas; on the other hand, he "domesticates" them and removes their challenging, difficult quality. The reality behind this contradiction, surely, is that Culler's clarity wins some converts, but that in so doing he exposes the inherent weaknesses of deconstruction to clearer view.

But there is still another contradiction here; on the one hand, we are told that the ideas inherent in deconstruction are challenging, disturbing, provocative (and if there is one constant in all the descriptions of and claims for deconstruction, it is this); but on the other hand, we are also told, in effect, that the nature of the challenge cannot be *precisely* stated, because that would remove the challenge. To this it must be said that any challenge is by its nature sharp, specific, and clear: a challenge without a well-placed thrust is not a challenge at all.

Once again, a crucial and instructive gap can be noticed in the objections to Culler: rarely is a specific example given of the "domestication" and of the damage it has done to a particular deconstructive idea. If one wants to say that Culler's translation of deconstruction into terms that can be understood by the American reader *change* it, one has the obligation to set out the two formulations side by side and demonstrate just what is lost in the transition from one to the other. In the absence of such a demonstration, the charge of "domestication" remains a generalized one that is repeated by one writer after another but never explained. I should point out here, however, that this reply to Culler's critics is only a very incomplete defense of him, since it leaves him open to a potentially more serious charge. For while it is true, on the one hand, that they have not shown, for example, what really is lost from "all interpretation is misinterpretation" when Culler restates it as "no interpretation is final," it is also true that the second view, as they imply, is shorn of intellectual interest; and it therefore remains something of a problem for Culler that, having explained deconstruction as he does, he still recommends its po-

[6] S. F. Rendall, review of *On Deconstruction*, in *Comparative Literature* 36 (1984), pp. 263–64.

sitions enthusiastically. In order to recommend deconstruction to others, Culler often makes clear in this way that
deconstruction advocates some very uninteresting positions;
why, then, would he think it worth recommending?

The inevitable result of this generalized resistance to any
change in or analysis of terms, as opposed to a showing that a
particular change involves particular losses in meaning, with
particular arguments addressed to those changes, can only be
a rejection of reason itself; Mas'd Zavarzadeh takes just that
position in his review of Culler's *The Pursuit of Signs*.[7] But
this is a very serious step indeed, one that must, if taken seriously, stop the whole argument dead. It implies that there can
be no discussion of deconstruction at all and no possibility of
arguing for or against a particular viewpoint, deconstruction
or any other, and thus no exposition, examination, or evaluation of any views or arguments.

One last aspect of the refusal to reformulate and thus to
analyze the formulation of the original deconstructive terms
must be mentioned, one final defensive barrier that skeptics
must break through. This consists in the aura of sophistication
with which those terms are invested and that makes it easier
to insist upon them if they are challenged. It is as if the ability
to work with those terms is the essential guarantee that one is
able to work on the high intellectual level required by the argument; from which it would follow that any wish to replace
or question them betrays a falling-off from the level of sophistication required to be in the argument at all. And so, once
again, the original terms are protected from challenge or scrutiny (still another reason why deconstructionists are nervous
about Jonathan Culler's willingness to leave those terms behind). The reply to this is, of course, the same one that we have
seen before: if the difference between the original terms and
the new ones is that the former are far more sophisticated than
the latter, it should be possible to show just how the extra
logical sophistication is lost; if we allow the generalized claim
to stand without the accompanying particular demonstration,

---

[7] *Journal of Aesthetics and Art Criticism* 40 (1982), pp. 329–33.

we have surrendered the only defense we have against swallowing the merely pretentious.

It follows that deconstructive logic makes its way not by any genuinely logical means but, instead, by its psychological appeal.[8] Deconstruction offers its followers much psychological satisfaction. Essential to its logic—not a by-product, as is the case where a substantial intellectual innovation really has taken place—is the sense of belonging to an intellectual elite, of having left behind the naiveté of the crowd, of operating on a more sophisticated intellectual plane than that crowd. I say essential, because the naiveté of the crowd is deconstruction's very starting point, and its subsequent move is as much an emotional as an intellectual leap to a position that *feels* different as much in the one way as the other. This is a powerful appeal. Curiously enough, while the deconstructionist feels rebellious, iconoclastic, and nonconformist, what strikes the outsider is the standardized, routine quality of the performance.[9] Expositions of the deconstructive terminology of "presence," "difference," etc., seem to be done in ritual fashion, as if a litany were being repeated, rather than in the probing, analytical, testing style one expects of scholars who are entering new, uncharted areas. And so a powerful sense of independence, originality, and intellectual progress is achieved without

[8] For some comments on the psychological appeal of deconstruction with a different emphasis, see Dennis Donoghue's review, of *Allegories of Reading*, by Paul de Man, *New York Review of Books*, (12 June 1980) and Harold Bloom, Paul de Man, Jacques Derrida, Geoffrey Hartman, and J. Hillis Miller, *Deconstruction and Criticism* (New York, 1979).

[9] Another way of looking at this point is to consider deconstruction in the context of the history of skeptical thought generally. Here an odd contrast emerges; for one typically experiences skeptics as lone dissenters, disturbed and perhaps even tormented by their doubts. Deconstruction is surely quite different; it is not hesitant but cheerfully and aggressively assertive—have real skeptics ever been so self-confident? And while skeptics have generally been riveted by their own individual convictions and isolated by them, deconstructionists acknowledge an authority, join a school of thought, and accept a body of doctrines. Graff, too ("Deconstruction as Dogma," *Georgia Review* 34 (1980), p. 409), notices the discrepancy between deconstruction's theoretical commitment to putting everything in question, on the one hand, and its assertive and self-assured form, on the other.

the hard work, continued effort, ingenuity, and skill that intellectual breakthroughs really require and without the individual risk that genuine independence must bring. Achieving real complexity of thought is immensely difficult: deconstruction provides a kind of formula, so that the kinds of psychological satisfaction it offers are achieved without the corresponding real achievements that normally must precede them. Anyone who has produced a new theory that has had enough *force* to be shocking (whatever the field) knows how difficult it is to work his way through to a new view that is well grounded enough to be genuinely shocking as opposed to dismissably crackpot. By contrast, deconstruction gives its adherents a routine way to a feeling of being excitingly shocking; and since this feeling usually comes only after a considerable intellectual feat, it is surely a highly desirable state of mind.

So much, then, for the shape and immediate appeal of deconstructive logic; but there still remains the wider question of its place within the theory and practice of criticism in the English-speaking world and of the factors that have made it prosper within that context. To this question I now turn in my final chapter.

CHAPTER SEVEN

Conclusion: The Meaning
of Deconstruction in the Contemporary
Critical Scene

ADVOCATES OF DECONSTRUCTION regularly make certain claims for it, both implicitly and explicitly. Most important is the claim that it is a bold, provocative, and innovative movement, which challenges the status quo with radical, disturbing ideas. A second claim is that it is heavily theoretical in nature and represents a more important place for theory in the critical scheme of things. And finally, a claim implicit in the deconstructionist's general rhetorical stance is that this new mode is far more sophisticated than anything in criticism heretofore. But, if I am correct, none of these claims withstands closer inspection. It is, first of all, not difficult to see that deconstruction's major themes had been a part of the critical scene long before its arrival there. Moreover, these were not peripheral or marginal issues but central features of the critical landscape; they have been and still are among the most important handicaps and liabilities especially of American criticism. In this chapter I shall argue that the only sense in which deconstruction can be said to represent change in the critical context lies in its giving a new shape and a renewed force and virulence to preexisting ideas and attitudes: it has given an appearance of theoretical sophistication to what had previously been the more or less incoherent attitudes and prejudices of majority practice. But this in turn would mean that deconstruction had, in effect, reversed the more usual role of theory.

"Theory of criticism" is surely best thought of not as a set of dogmas but rather as an activity—the activity of analyzing, reflecting on, and thinking through the current practices of criticism to uncover its possible inconsistencies and insufficiencies and to improve on those parts of it that cannot stand up to careful analysis. In deconstruction, for all the rhetoric of probing and examining, this schema is really reversed: suddenly the persistent, stubbornly held attitudes that were formerly threatened by theoretical analysis take on the cloak of theory itself. Now "theory" becomes in large measure a new vehicle through which older, unthinking attitudes are clung to and genuine change resisted.[1]

If we attempt to abstract the most persistent and widely held conceptions of the character of criticism and critical activity in the English-speaking world, the results will surely be anything but the belief in the single, clear, statable textual meaning that is deconstruction's target. The most prevalent view has been quite the reverse: criticism is not like science and does not lead to clear, objective results. Good criticism is stimulating rather than true, and since stimulation can occur in many different ways, that would make its character quite unlike that of the unitary scientific truth. Criticism, it is said, illuminates texts from many angles, and many quite different critical perspectives can all be of value in their own way. All can "shed light" on the text—but different kinds of light. Critics, then, are legitimately different, and that in turn has meant that the critic's individual character and personality are an important element of criticism. The point of good criticism cannot lie in its discovering *the* meaning of a text; to use that criterion would be to return to the unitary truths of science. The critic's individual temperament and viewpoint are a factor, and so his imagination and creativity must be in evidence. This very common view accords critics a great deal of free-

---

[1] All of this means that the character of deconstruction in its French origin is quite different from that of its American adoption. In France, deconstruction is part of a revolt against an extremely narrow rationalist tradition in criticism and, more broadly, in cultural life. To be sure, this revolt had also become somewhat stereotyped in French intellectual life before Derrida arrived to give it one more shape; and there remains the problem of the incoherence and ineffectiveness of Derrida's version. But the fact remains that there was a real antiestablishment element in French deconstruction, while the American counterpart represents only a new way to cling to an old set of attitudes.

dom. Individuals may be affected by the literary work in different ways and therefore must be free to pursue different paths. This in turn introduces a reluctance to say that one response to a text may be right and another simply wrong; instead there is a tendency to allow that each is illuminating different facets of the work. Criticism is judged less by the force of its argument than by the qualities of critical imagination it displays and by the stimulus it gives to the reader's own imagination. In this climate of opinion,[2] attempts to show that a particular piece of criticism does not meet necessary standards—say, standards of intellectual coherence or of relevance to the actual terms and emphases of the text under discussion—are usually thought of as being intolerant of a necessary critical pluralism and inappropriately dogmatic where certainty is not available.

To be sure, literary historians and biographers had always argued that the background information they uncovered provided objective evidence for the text's meaning. But what has recently been forgotten is that this insistence on the unique value of background information arose precisely from the prevailing skepticism as to the text's inherent power to convey a particular meaning. The reason why one had to cling to hard information about the author's social and personal situation, so the argument ran, was that, taken simply by themselves, literary texts could mean whatever their readers saw in them. Historical and biographical critics not only shared in the prevailing consensus on the language of the text being open to any interpretation and response if taken only by itself, they needed that consensus and used it as the essential basis of and justification for their position.

The prevailing critical consensus, then, has long insisted on pluralism, on the value of different critical viewpoints, and on criticism's lacking the character of science. I do not wish to go into the question of the logical adequacy of this view here but

[2] The prevailing "laissez-faire" and "wise eclecticism" of criticism were described and discussed in my *The Theory of Literary Criticism* (Berkeley, 1974); that description is as relevant now as it was in the decades preceding this book.

must note one practical disadvantage of it that annoys most critics whether or not they have understood that this unfortunate result derives ultimately from the randomly pluralistic, theoretical consensus that they help to preserve: the problem that annoys everyone is the flood of critical writing, the general level of which is widely acknowledged to be much less than inspiring. This is, surely, the likely consequence of a situation where there is more emphasis on the sanctity of the individual critic's right to see things as he sees them, than on the need to insist on the strength of an argument as the major standard by which to judge the value of criticism. If no one cares to talk about standards for intelligent criticism, then the content and value of published criticism will vary enormously—and it does; and well-nigh everyone, including the most ardent advocates of theoretically unrestrained pluralism, is unhappy with at least some aspects of this situation. And so the situation remains one in which most critics become uncomfortable with any determined attempt to demonstrate that a particular interpretation fits the evidence of the text in a compelling way or, conversely, that another interpretation is so inconsistent with the text that it can simply be rejected.[3] The point here is not that they do or do not like the interpretations concerned but that they prefer to think of critical arguments as all making a contribution, with perhaps some

[3] Gerald Graff observes in his review of Geoffrey Hartman's *Criticism in the Wilderness* (*The New Republic*, 1 November 1980) that deconstruction's ironizing of everything "echoes an older, genteel academic code of manners, which looked on all 'serious' postures as unseemly and unbefitting a gentleman. One sometimes wonders if for all its celebrated ferocity and its self-proclaimed appetite for risk, recent avant-garde criticism is not decorously conservative at bottom." Though the emphasis here is on gentility and gentlemanliness, while my own is more on the resistance to accountability, it appears to me that we are both talking about the same underlying phenomenon: deconstruction's playing to the strong conservative current in criticism that resists the sense of criticism's being a public activity and a shared inquiry rather than simply an individual expression. In another review of this book (*Modern Language Review* 77, 1982, pp. 439–40) A. D. Nuttall also sees that, in spite of his professed wish that criticism should be more hospitable to theory, "the main thrust of his [Hartman's] argument is anti-theoretical, in that it opposes explanation as such."

more than others, rather than some failing while others succeed. (The underlying logical problem here is, of course, once more the implicit choice between final objectivity and mere subjectivity: either we have the final, absolute truth about a text or there is only individual opinion with none, in principle, superior to others.)

This prevailing climate of American criticism, whose watchword was pluralism, scarcely provided a well-guarded citadel that deconstructionists needed to conquer by force; on the contrary, nothing could have been more receptive to deconstruction's major themes than a situation that was already very close to them. All that was needed was a change of formulation. The older stress on the legitimacy of differing critical viewpoints easily translates into textuality and reader-response criticism; the prior resistance to any idea of objectivity in criticism easily absorbs the idea that all readings are misreadings; the stress on the individual critic's imagination and creativity finds its counterpart in the deconstructive breaking down of the distinction between literature and criticism;[4] the inexhaustibility of the text can easily handle the infinity of meaning in the endless play of signs. Advocates of deconstruction are dreaming if they really believe that this thrust runs radically counter to, and disturbs, the entrenched attitudes of American criticism. Deconstruction's success in America is, in fact, explained by just the reverse—by its playing to the prevailing climate and giving that climate a new air of legitimacy.

So much for the allegedly radical nature of deconstruction's thrust; but now what of its status as theory? Here, too, there is much to be skeptical of in deconstruction's claim to represent a triumph of theory or a heightened place for theory in

---

[4] Compare, for example, R. Spiller, p. 55 of "Literary History," in *The Aims and Methods of Scholarship in Modern Languages and Literature*, ed. James Thorpe (New York, 1963) with Eugenio Donato, p. 95 of "The Two Languages of Criticism," in *The Structuralist Controversy*, ed. Richard Macksey and Eugenio Donato (Baltimore and London, 1972). Spiller in 1963 speaks of the "insights and aesthetic controls of the artist—in this case the literary historian," while Donato later, in the deconstructive era, tells us that "Derrida's enterprise also reveals within our modern context the impossibility of drawing an essential line between literature and criticism."

the world of criticism. This is not just a matter of deconstruction's being bad, incoherent theory in that a genuinely theoretical argument ought to be much more than one that plays with opposed extreme views and ought to employ analysis rather than rhetorical drama. The deeper problem, however, is that deconstruction's major themes are themselves *inherently antitheoretical* in nature.

Take, for example, the freedom that textuality grants to readers, critics, and texts. Critics are given freedom to read texts without constraint, texts can mean an infinity of meanings, and readers use unrestrained creativity to discover meaning. Now theorists, by their very nature, do not grant this kind of license to people or situations to do or be whatever they wish; theory always moves in the opposite direction. Nor do theorists generally reach such an easy peace with the strong undercurrents of the status quo of a field as deconstruction's accommodation with the prevalent laissez-faire of critical practice. Typically, theorists analyze situations to investigate the relations between different aspects of current beliefs and practices and reach conclusions about the relative coherence or incoherence of ideas. That kind of analysis will always exert pressure on particular aspects of the status quo, a pressure that will introduce new restraints more than it will abolish them. By contrast, the kind of thinking that tends towards removing such restraints represents a resistance to making distinctions and so a resistance to any real scope for theoretical analysis.

Theory exerts its pressure on the status quo by continual examination of the basis and rationale for the accepted activities of a field of study. Inevitably, the results will in principle be quite unlike the usual deconstructive attitudes: they should not leave us with issues and activities more undefined than ever but instead introduce a clarification and differentiation of fundamentally different kinds of activities. The consequence of this kind of activity will generally be a pressure to rearrange priorities; by its very nature, then, theory is indeed disturbing. But theoretical argument must for that very reason proceed with great care. It must be above all a careful, patient, analytical process: its strengths must lie in precision of formulation, in well-drawn distinctions, in carefully delineated concepts. In theoretical discourse, argument is met by argument; one careful attempt to analyze and elucidate the basis of a critical concept or position is met by an equally exacting and penetrating scrutiny of its own inner logic. That makes theoretical argument very much a communal process: there is no room in it for individual license, for claims of exemption from logical scrutiny, for appeals to an undefined unique logical status, for appeals to allow obscurity to stand unanalyzed, or for freedom to do as one wishes.

The most enduring fault of literary criticism as a field has been its readiness to abandon the communal sense of a shared inquiry, in which individual perceptions are expected to be tested and sifted by others. A shared inquiry means a commitment to argument and dialogue, while a criticism that insists on the value of each individual critic's perspective, in effect, refuses to make that commitment. Before deconstruction, theory of criticism worked against the laissez-faire tendencies of criticism; but now deconstruction, an intensified expression of those tendencies, has attempted to seize the mantle of theory in order to pursue this antitheoretical program.[5] The result is an apparent novelty that, looked at more closely, consists in resistance to change and, more particularly, to that change that is most urgently needed: the development of some check on and control of the indigestible, chaotic flow of critical writing through reflection on what is and what is not in principle worthwhile—that is, through genuine, rather than illusory, theoretical reflection.

[5] While there may be some truth to the view taken by, for example, R. Cairns Craig ("Review Article: Criticism and the Truths of Literature," *Dalhousie Review*, 1980 p. 527) that deconstruction is "precisely suited to the conditions of literary 'research' in the graduate school: Learn the technique, choose your author, follow out the deconstructions," I think that there are broader, and ultimately deeper, and more important causes of deconstruction's appeal. In general, then, I look to the long-standing and continuing character of literary criticism for the causes of this phenomenon rather than to more local and recent political or social factors.

Bibliography

Abrams, M. H. "The Deconstructive Angel." *Critical Inquiry* 3 (1977), pp. 425–38.

Arac, Jonathan, Wlad Godzich, and Wallace Martin, eds. *The Yale Critics: Deconstruction in America.* Minneapolis, 1983.

Bass, Alan. " 'Literature'/Literature." In *Velocities of Change*, edited by Richard Macksey. Baltimore and London, 1974.

Benveniste, Emile. *Problèmes de Linguistique Générale.* Paris, 1966.

Bersani, Leo. "From Bachelard to Barthes." *Partisan Review* 34 (1967), pp. 215–32.

Bloom, Harold. *The Anxiety of Influence: A Theory of Poetry.* Oxford, 1973.

———. *A Map of Misreading.* Oxford, 1975.

Bloom, Harold, et al. *Deconstruction and Criticism.* New York, 1979.

Brooks, Peter. "Savant of Signs." *The New Republic* (11 November 1982), pp. 27–31.

Cain, William. *The Crisis in Criticism: Theory, Literature, and Reform in English Studies.* Baltimore and London, 1984.

———. "Deconstruction in America: The Recent Literary Criticism of J. Hillis Miller." *College English* 41 (1979), pp. 367–82.

Campbell, Colin. "The Tyranny of the Yale Critics." *New York Times Magazine* (9 February 1986), pp. 20–48.

Craig, R. Cairns. "Review Article: Criticism and the Truths of Literature." *Dalhousie Review* 60 (1980), pp. 517–35.

Crews, Frederick. "In the Big House of Theory." *New York Review of Books* (29 May 1986), pp. 36–42.

Crosman, Robert. "Do Readers Make Meaning?" In *The Reader in the Text: Essays on Audience and Interpretation*, edited by Susan R. Suleiman and Inge Crosman. Princeton, 1980.

Culler, Jonathan. *Ferdinand de Saussure.* Harmondsworth, 1977.

———. *On Deconstruction: Theory and Criticism after Structuralism.* Ithaca, 1982.

———. *The Pursuit of Signs.* Ithaca, 1981.

———. *Structuralist Poetics.* Ithaca, 1976.

de Man, Paul. *Allegories of Reading: Figural Language in Rousseau, Nietzsche, Rilke and Proust.* New Haven, 1979.

———. *Blindness and Insight.* 2d ed. Minneapolis, 1983.

————. "Nietzsche's Theory of Rhetoric." *Symposium* 28 (1974), pp. 33–51.

Derrida, Jacques. *Dissemination*. Translated by Barbara Johnson. Chicago, 1981.

————. *Margins of Philosophy*. Translated by Alan Bass. Chicago, 1982.

————. "Limited, Inc. abc." *Glyph* 2 (1977), pp. 162–254.

————. *The Post Card: From Socrates to Freud*. Translated by Alan Bass. Chicago, 1987.

————. *Of Grammatology*. Translated by Gayatri Chakravorty Spivak. Baltimore, 1976.

————. *Positions*. Translated by Alan Bass. Chicago, 1981.

————. "Signature, Event, Context." *Glyph* 1 (1977), pp. 172–97.

————. *Glas*. Translated by John P. Leavey, Jr. Lincoln, Nebr., 1986.

————. *Speech and Phenomena*. Translated by David Allison. Evanston, 1973.

————. *Signéponge: Signsponge*. Translated by Richard Rand. New York, 1984.

————. *Writing and Difference*. Translated by Alan Bass. Chicago, 1978.

Dilthey, Wilhelm. *Einleitung in die Geisteswissenschaften*. Berlin, 1883.

Donato, Eugenio. "The Two Languages of Criticism." In *The Structuralist Controversy: The Languages of Criticism and the Sciences of Man*, edited by Richard Macksey and Eugenio Donato. Baltimore and London, 1972.

Donoghue, Dennis. "Deconstructing Deconstruction." *New York Review of Books* (12 June 1980), pp. 37–41.

Ellis, John M. *Heinrich von Kleist: Studies in the Character and Meaning of His Writings*. Chapel Hill, 1979.

————. *The Theory of Literary Criticism: A Logical Analysis*. Berkeley, 1974.

————. "Wittgensteinian Thinking in Theory of Criticism." *New Literary History* 12 (1981), pp. 437–52.

Firth, John Rupert. *Papers in Linguistics 1934–1951*. Oxford, 1957.

————. *"The Tongues of Men" and "Speech."* Oxford, 1964.

————. *Selected Papers of J. R. Firth, 1952–1959*. Edited by F. R. Palmer. Bloomington, 1968.

Fischer, Michael. *Does Deconstruction Make Any Difference?* Bloomington, 1985.

————. Review of *Wittgenstein and Derrida*, by Henry Staten. *Philosophy and Literature* 10 (1986), pp. 93–97.

Fish, Stanley. *Is There a Text in This Class?* Cambridge, 1980.

Flieger, Jerry Aline. "The Art of Being Taken by Surprise." *SCE Reports* 8 (Fall 1980), pp. 54–67.

Gasché, Rodolphe. "Deconstruction as Criticism." *Glyph* 6 (1979), pp. 177–215.

Ghose, Sisirkumar. "Mysticism." *Encyclopaedia Britannica*, 15th ed., Macropaedia: 12, 786–93.

Goethe, Johann W. *Goethes Werke*. Edited by Erich Trunz. 14 vols. Hamburg, 1948–1960.

Graff, Gerald. "Culler and Deconstruction." *London Review of Books* (3–16 September 1981), pp. 7–8.

———. "Deconstruction as Dogma, or, 'Come Back to the Raft Ag'in, Strether Honey!'" *Georgia Review* 34 (1980), pp. 404–21.

———. *Literature Against Itself*. Chicago, 1979.

———. "The Pseudo Politics of Interpretation." *Critical Inquiry* 9 (1983), pp. 597–610.

———. Review of *Criticism in the Wilderness*, by Geoffrey Hartman. *The New Republic* (1 November 1980), pp. 34–37.

Hartman, Geoffrey. *Criticism in the Wilderness*. Yale, 1980.

Hawkes, Terence. *Structuralism and Semiotics*. Berkeley and Los Angeles, 1977.

Iser, Wolfgang. *Der Akt des Lesens*. Munich, 1976. Translated under the title *The Act of Reading*. Baltimore and London, 1978.

———. *Der implizite Leser*. Munich, 1972. Translated under the title *The Implied Reader*. Baltimore and London, 1974.

Jameson, Fredric. *The Prison House of Language. A Critical Account of Structuralism and Russian Formalism*. Princeton, 1972.

Johnson, Barbara. *The Critical Difference*. Baltimore, 1980.

———. "Nothing Fails Like Success." *SCE Reports* 8 (Fall 1980), pp. 7–16.

Kurz, Gerhard. Review of *Allegories of Reading*, by Paul de Man. *Arbitrium* 1 (1985), pp. 6–11.

Lentricchia, Frank. *After the New Criticism*. Chicago, 1980.

Leitch, Vincent. "The Book of Deconstructive Criticism." *Studies in the Literary Imagination* 12 (1979), pp. 22–25.

———. *Deconstructive Criticism*. New York, 1983.

———. "The Lateral Dance: The Deconstructive Criticism of J. Hillis Miller." *Critical Inquiry* 6 (1980), pp. 593–607.

McFadden, George. Review of *Allegories of Reading*, by Paul de Man. *Journal of Aesthetics and Art Criticism* 39 (1981), pp. 337–41.

McGlathery, James. "Desire's Persecutions in Kafka's 'Judgement,' 'Metamorphosis,' and 'A Country Doctor.' " *Perspectives in Contemporary Literature* 7 (1981), pp. 54–63.

———. *Desire's Sway: The Plays and Stories of Heinrich von Kleist.* Detroit, 1983.

———. *Mysticism and Sexuality: E.T.A. Hoffman.* Las Vegas, Berne, and Frankfort/Main, 1981.

Macksey, Richard, ed. *Velocities of Change.* Baltimore and London, 1974.

Macksey, Richard, and Eugenio Donato, eds. *The Structuralist Controversy: The Languages of Criticism and the Sciences of Man.* Baltimore and London, 1972.

Melzer, Sara E. Review of *The Post Card*, by Jacques Derrida. *Los Angeles Times* (12 July 1987), p. 6.

Miller, J. Hillis. "Deconstructing the Deconstructors." *Diacritics* 5 (1975), pp. 24–31.

———. "How Deconstruction Works." *New York Times Magazine* (9 February 1986), p. 25.

Nietzsche, Friedrich. "Uber Wahrheit und Lüge im aussermoralischen Sinne." *Nietzsche: Werke, Kritische Gesamtausgabe.* Edited by Georgio Colli and Mazzino Montinari. (Berlin and New York, 1973), pt. 3, vol. 2, pp. 369–84.

Norris, Christopher: *The Deconstructive Turn: Essays in the Rhetoric of Philosophy.* London and New York, 1983.

———. *Deconstruction: Theory and Practice.* London and New York, 1982.

Nuttall, A. D. Review of *Criticism in the Wilderness*, by Geoffrey Hartman. *Modern Language Review* 77 (1982), pp. 439–40.

Peirce, Charles Saunders. *Collected Papers.* Vols. 1–6. Edited by Charles Hartshorne and Paul Weiss. Vols. 7–8. Edited by Arthur Burks. Cambridge, Mass., 1931–1958.

Rendall, Steven. "Mus in Pice: Montaigne and Interpretation." *MLN* 94 (1979), pp. 1056–71.

———. Review of *On Deconstruction*, by Jonathan Culler; *Deconstructive Criticism*, by Vincent Leitch; and *The Yale Critics*, edited by Jonathan Arac, Wlad Godzich, and Wallace Martin. *Comparative Literature* 36 (1984), pp. 263–38.

Riddel, Joseph N. *The Inverted Bell: Modernism and the Counterpoetics of William Carlos Williams.* Baton Rouge, 1974.

———. "What Is Deconstruction, and Why Are They Writing All Those Graff-ic Things About It?" *SCE Reports* 8 (Fall 1980), pp. 17–29.

Sapir, Edward. *Language.* New York, 1921.

Saussure, Ferdinand de. *Cours de Linguistique Générale.* Edited by Charles Bally, Albert Sechahaye, and Albert Riedinger. New edition by Tullio de Mauro. Paris, 1981. Translated by Wade Baskin, under the title *Course in General Linquistics.* New York, 1959.

Scholes, Robert. *Textual Power: Literary Theory and the Teaching of English.* New Haven, 1985.

Searle, John R. "Reiterating the Differences: A Reply to Derrida." *Glyph* 1 (1977), pp. 198–208.

———. "The Word Turned Upside Down." *New York Review of Books* (27 October 1983), pp. 73–79.

Spanos, William V. "Retrieving Heidegger's De-Struction: A Response to Barbara Johnson." *SEC Reports* 8 (Fall 1980), pp. 30–53.

Spiller, R. "Literary History." In *The Aims and Methods of Scholarship in Modern Languages and Literatures*, edited by James Thorpe. New York, 1963.

Staten, Henry. *Wittgenstein and Derrida.* Lincoln, Nebr., and London, 1984.

Sturrock, John, ed. *Structuralism and Since.* Oxford, 1979.

Sturrock, John. Review of *Deconstruction: Theory and Practice*, by Christopher Norris. *Times Literary Supplement* (9 July 1982), p. 734.

Suleiman, Susan R., and Inge Crosman, eds. *The Reader in the Text: Essays on Audience and Interpretation.* Princeton, 1980.

Thorpe, James, ed. *The Aims and Methods of Scholarship in Modern Languages and Literatures.* New York, 1963.

Tompkins, Jane P. "An Introduction to Reader Response Criticism." In *Reader-Response Criticism: From Formalism to Post-Structuralism*, edited by Jane P. Tompkins. Baltimore and London, 1980.

Whorf, Benjamin Lee. *Language, Thought, and Reality. Selected Writings of Benjamin Lee Whorf.* Edited by John B. Carroll. Cambridge, Mass., 1956.

Wimsatt, William K., and Monroe Beardsley. "The Intentional Fallacy." In *The Verbal Icon: Studies in the Meaning of Poetry.* Lexington, 1954.

Wittgenstein, Ludwig. *Philosophical Investigations.* Translated by G.E.M. Anscombe. 3d ed. New York, 1958.

Zavarzadeh, Mas'd. Review of *The Pursuit of Signs*, by Jonathan Culler. *Journal of Aesthetics and Art Criticism* 40 (1982), pp. 329–33.

Index